THE
Quick After-Work
Vegetarian
COOKBOOK

Other titles by Judy Ridgway, also published by Piatkus

The Quick After-Work Pasta Cookbook
Vegetarian Delights
The Complete Cheese Cookbook

THE
Quick After-Work
Vegetarian
COOKBOOK

Judy Ridgway

PIATKUS

ACKNOWLEDGEMENTS

The publishers would like to thank the following organisations for
supplying photographs for use in this book:

The British Egg Information Bureau
US Quality Bean Information Bureau
Food and Wine from France

First published in 1994 by
Judy Piatkus (Publishers) Limited
5 Windmill Street, London W1P 1HF

Reprinted 1994
Reprinted 1995
First paperback edition 1995

The moral right of the author has been asserted

*A catalogue record for this book
is available from the British Library*

ISBN 0 7499 1390 8 (Hbk)
ISBN 0 7499 1532 3 (Pbk)

Designed by Paul Saunders
Illustrations by Madeleine David
Photographs opposite pages 26 and 123 by Martin Brigdale

Front cover photograph shows Mixed Vegetables with Cashews (page 127)
and Singapore Noodles (page 147)

Back cover photograph shows Orange and Mozzarella Salad with
Chervil (page 40) and Tuscan Chickpea Soup with Pasta (page 10)

Typeset by Phoenix Photosetting, Chatham, Kent
Printed and bound in Great Britain by
Mackays of Chatham PLC, Chatham, Kent

CONTENTS

INTRODUCTION

RATHER than having more leisure in the 1990s I seem to have less! I am lucky to be working, but, like nearly everyone else I know, I am working longer hours and coming home later. Once home I just want to flop down in front of the television or, on more energetic evenings, there are evening classes, training sessions or sports matches to attend.

What I do not want to do is spend much time – or indeed use up my remaining energy – slaving away in the kitchen. Therefore I need easy but attractive meals which can be prepared in half an hour or so. This is not as unrealistic as it might sound. I have spent the last four or five months working on recipes and menus which fulfil these criteria and this book is the result of that work.

Some people think that vegetarian food takes longer to prepare than 'meat and two veg' but you'll see that this is just not true. All the recipes in the book can be prepared in about half an hour, and many are ready to eat in a good deal less time. This means that a two course meal with fruit to finish can be made very quickly indeed.

Although I sometimes cook the whole evening meal from ingredients bought that day, more often I mix fresh ingredients with canned, bottled or frozen foods that I have in the storecupboard and freezer. A really interesting stock of ingredients can help considerably in turning readily available every-day food into a real feast.

I am very fortunate to have a variety of ethnic stores and specialist deli-catessens within easy reach of my home, but wherever I am, I never pass an interesting food shop or go to a food show without looking for things to add to my store. For example, my latest purchases were a jar of grilled and marinated baby onions in olive oil, some caper berries and a large bottle of pickled lemons from Spain – I am still learning how to use the latter to best advantage.

My storecupboard also contains a wide selection of basics so that I never get fed up with the same type of pasta, and I can substitute couscous, bulgar or polenta for rice whenever I feel like it. There are also plenty of dried and canned beans and peas and a selection of nuts and seeds. I have given suggestions for what to keep in your storecupboard on page 4.

Deciding on the menu for the evening only takes a minute or two and is inspired either by the contents of the storecupboard or my vegetable rack, or by the fruit and vegetables on sale at road stalls, markets and supermarket on the way to and from my office. Some of the most successful two-course combinations developed during the testing of this book are given on page 5.

I usually use fresh herbs, and have done so for all the recipes in this book, except where stated. The dishes are intended to serve four, but as appetites vary you may find they will feed more or fewer people. Throughout the book, recipes suitable for vegans are marked with a Ⓥ.

I do hope that this book will encourage everyone who has to produce quick after-work meals to experiment with different ingredients and only use the supermarket chiller cabinet in an emergency!

EATING A BALANCED DIET

There is no reason why eating a diet free from meat and fish should not be as healthy and nutritious as any other. All the nutrients you need can easily be obtained from vegetarian foods. Indeed, vegetarians are better placed than most to follow the current healthy eating guidelines.

Provided that you do not rely too heavily on dairy produce there is very little saturated fat to avoid and the diet is naturally rich in carbohydrate foods such as pasta, bread, potatoes, beans and lentils. There are also plenty of protein-rich vegetables such as dried and canned beans, nuts and seeds, rice, bread, pasta and oatmeal.

If some of these protein foods are eaten together you will gain even more protein than if you eat them separately. One of the best of these combinations is cereals and pulses; examples include baked beans on toast, hummus with pitta bread, rice cooked with beans, peanut butter sandwiches and taco shells filled with lentils or re-fried beans. These combinations are particularly important for vegans who do not eat eggs or cheese.

A vegetarian diet should also be rich in fresh fruit and vegetables and this will ensure that you getting plenty of vitamins and minerals. However, it is important to understand that iron from vegetable sources is more effectively absorbed in the presence of Vitamin C. Good combinations here include toast and orange juice at breakfast and watercress and orange salad with other meals.

Vegans may need to think about giving their children more calcium-rich foods such as almonds, sesame seeds, whole bread and spring greens and vitamin B12-enriched soya milk or breakfast cereals.

The easiest way to eat a balanced diet is to eat as many different kinds of food as possible. Experiment with unusual cereals such as polenta (yellow cornmeal), couscous, bulgar and quinoa as well as with soy products like tofu, miso and tempeh. Try yeast extracts, seaweed and tahina paste. Mix all of these with more everyday items like potatoes, bread, cheese, carrots, apples and oranges.

Even if you regularly grab a quick snack or prepare the whole meal in half an hour, try to do something different every day. Do not just rely on a small number of tried and trusted dishes. The more you experiment the wider your range will become and the more nutritious your meals will be.

VEGETARIAN CHEESE

An increasing number of cheeses are being made with vegetarian coagulants of various kinds. There are rennet-free versions of most of the traditional English cheeses and some of the continental classics. In addition, many of the new wave of English farmhouse soft cheeses are made without rennet. If the cheese is not labelled or you are not sure how it is made, buy only from a cheese specialist who should be able to tell you all you need to know about each cheese-maker's production methods.

THE STORECUPBOARD

Here's an idea of what I always keep in the storecupboard.

BASIC INGREDIENTS
These are the staple ingredients which form the base of many of my quick after-work meals:

- Long pasta – spaghetti, spaghettini and fettucine
- Pasta shapes – bows, fusilli and rigatoni
- Chinese egg noodles and Japanese buckwheat noodles
- Rice – basmati, long-grain and risotto
- Quick-cook polenta (yellow cornmeal)
- Bulgar
- Couscous
- Canned kidney beans, chickpeas and cannelini beans
- Dried lentils
- Canned tomatoes and tomato purée
- Frozen peas, sweetcorn and asparagus
- Vegetable stock cubes and yeast extract
- Soy and Tabasco sauces
- Sunflower and olive oils

INTERESTING FLAVOURING INGREDIENTS
This list includes items that I use to provide inspiration for, and add interest to dishes:

- A variety of herbs and spices
- Dried wild mushrooms
- Sun-dried tomatoes – packed in oil, dry and paste
- Pesto sauce
- Horseradish sauce
- Green and black olives – whole and paste
- Capers
- Peanut butter
- Flaked almonds and pine nuts
- Sunflower, sesame and pumpkin seeds
- Chinese black bean sauce
- Chinese plum sauce
- Vegetarian Worcestershire sauce
- Sesame oils, plain and toasted
- Curry powder
- Sherry and balsamic vinegars

MENU SUGGESTIONS

Here are some two-course combinations for quick meals. The desserts are up to you.

Cauliflower with Guacamole(V)
*
Spicy Corn Pilaf with Banana Kebabs(V)

Celeriac and Carrot Soup(V)
*
Leek and Walnut Omelette
Chicory Spears filled with Cucumber Hummus and pitta bread

Chickpeas with Spinach(V)
*
Welsh Rarebit

Orange and Date Salad(V)
*
Broad Beans and Okra Couscous
A green salad

Avocado Salad with Hot Grapefruit Sauce
*
Polenta Rustica
Courgette Salad(V)

Aubergine and Mozzarella Bruschetta
*
Bean and Celery Soup(V)

Warm Carrot Salad with Rocket(V)
*
Grilled Aubergines with Olive Paste and Tomatoes(V)
Liptauer Cheese with sweet and sour cucumbers

Chilled Beetroot and Orange Soup
*
Pasta Bows with Goat's Cheese Sauce
Courgette Moulded Salad(V)

Tofu and Watercress Pâté with toast(V)
*
Lentil Burgers with Beans Provençale(V)
Apple, Date and Chicory Salad(V)

Red Pepper Salad(V)
*
Egyptian Rice with Falafel(V)
A tomato salad

CHAPTER ONE

SOUPS

SOUPS make a very good start to a meal but I used to think that it was necessary to cook them for a long time to concentrate the flavour, so they rarely appeared on my table mid-week. However, during the testing for this book I have discovered that quite the opposite is true. With the right ingredients, really well flavoured soups can be produced in a short time.

Some of the hot soups, such as Leek and Potato and Tuscan Chickpea Soup with Pasta, are thick and filling and only need to be accompanied by wholemeal bread to turn them into a main course. You might also add rice or bulgar to the soup as they do in the Southern States of America.

Cold soups are attractive in hot weather but if the meal has to be ready in half an hour there is no time to chill a cooked soup. The answer is to make soups that do not need to be cooked, using fruit and vegetables such as melon, cucumber and tomatoes. You will also benefit from the higher vitamin content.

When you have a little time to spare it is well worth making a double quantity of any of these soups, as, with the exception of Stracciatella, they all freeze well. On another occasion you will then have a ready-prepared first course to help you to prepare a full meal even faster.

Celeriac and Carrot Soup ⓥ

These two root vegetables work well together to produce a really sweet and velvety soup. There is no need for any extra herbs or spices. Just a good extra virgin olive oil and some really fresh vegetables.

1 small onion, peeled and chopped
2 tablespoons extra virgin olive oil
350g (12oz) celeriac, peeled and
  chopped

3 large carrots, peeled and chopped
salt and freshly ground black pepper
750–900ml (1¹/₄–1¹/₂ pints) vegetable
  stock

1. Gently fry the onion in the olive oil to soften but not brown.

2. Add the celeriac and carrots and cook very gently for about 3–4 minutes, stirring all the time.

3. Add the seasonings and stock and bring to the boil. Cover with a lid and reduce the heat. Simmer for 15–20 minutes until the vegetables are tender.

4. Purée in a blender or processor or rub through a sieve. Reheat and serve.

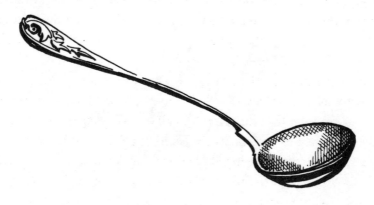

Leek and Potato Soup

This is just the kind of old-fashioned soup which seems to get forgotten these days. I prefer it in its chunky, unblended form but it does also make a very good smooth soup. If you have time to chill it you can very easily pass this soup off as *Vichyssoise*. Simply add plenty of cream and a handful of freshly chopped chives.

---•---

6 medium-sized leeks, trimmed and
   sliced into rings
25g (1oz) butter
450g (1lb) potatoes, peeled and diced

750ml (1¼ pints) vegetable stock
about 150ml (¼ pint) milk
salt and freshly ground black pepper

---•---

1. Gently fry the leeks in the butter to soften them. Add the potatoes and stir.

2. Pour on the stock and bring to the boil. Reduce the heat, cover and simmer for 15 minutes.

3. Add the milk, using a little more if the mixture is very thick. Season and cook for a further 5 minutes.

Coriander and Potato Soup Ⓥ

I have lived and worked in London's Bayswater for many years and in that time have seen a great change in the local populace. When I first came the peoples of central Europe were predominant with Poles and Hungarians vying for the best seats in the cafés. Now the Middle East has taken over.

The Lebanese greengrocer near my flat always has mountains of fresh, green coriander leaves and I have become addicted to their spicy flavour. I have used them in this simple potato soup to give an interesting twist.

———— • ————

2 cloves garlic, peeled and sliced
1 onion, peeled and sliced
1 tablespoon olive oil
1 × 225g (8oz) can tomatoes
700g (1½ lb) potatoes, peeled and
   diced
750ml (1¼ pints) vegetable stock or
   water

pinch dried oregano
1 whole green chilli
salt and freshly ground black pepper
4 tablespoons coarsely chopped fresh
   coriander leaves
juice of ½ lemon

———— • ————

1. In a saucepan, fry the garlic and onion in the olive oil for 4–5 minutes to lightly brown.

2. Add the tomatoes and their juice, the potatoes, stock, oregano, whole chilli, seasoning and 1 tablespoon of the coriander.

3. Bring to the boil. Cover and simmer for 15–20 minutes until the potatoes are cooked.

4. Remove the chilli. Spoon the soup into bowls and sprinkle with lemon juice and the rest of the coriander.

Tuscan Chickpea Soup with Pasta ⓥ

This is a thick heartwarming soup from Poggi Bonzi in the Chianti Classico area of Tuscany. The locals pour it over thick hunks of country bread and then add plenty of extra virgin olive oil.

———— • ————

1 × 400g (14oz) can chickpeas, drained
1 × 400g (14oz) can chopped tomatoes
750ml (1¼ pints) vegetable stock
4 tablespoons extra virgin olive oil, plus extra to serve

1 clove garlic, crushed
¼ teaspoon dried rosemary
1 tablespoon tomato purée
freshly ground black pepper
50g (2oz) soup pasta

———— • ————

1. Purée the chickpeas and tomatoes and their juice in a blender or food processor. Stir in the stock.

2. Gently fry the garlic in the olive oil for 1–2 minutes. Do not allow it to brown. Add the puréed vegetables, rosemary, tomato purée and seasoning.

3. Bring the soup to the boil and simmer for 5 minutes. Add the pasta and cook for another 10 minutes. Serve with extra virgin olive oil.

Bean and Celery Soup ⓥ

This is another soup typical of central Tuscany. No herbs are added and the soup depends for its flavour on first class olive oil, so buy the best extra virgin oil you can afford.

———— • ————

1 small onion, peeled and sliced
½ small head of celery, trimmed and sliced
2 tablespoons extra virgin olive oil, plus extra for serving

200g (7oz) canned red kidney beans, drained
750ml (1¼ pints) vegetable stock
salt and freshly ground black pepper

1. Gently fry the onion and celery in the olive oil for 4–5 minutes until the vegetables start to soften but do not allow them to become too brown.

2. Add the remaining ingredients and bring to the boil. Cover and simmer for 20 minutes.

3. Either serve the soup as it is or purée it in a food processor or blender, then reheat. Offer more extra virgin olive oil for diners to add to their soup.

Brussels Sprouts Soup Ⓥ

Sprouts are very widely available throughout the winter but they are rarely used in soups. This seems rather a pity when their flavour is so popular.

I have tried making this soup both with and without the chestnuts and I cannot make up my mind which I prefer! Try it both ways and make your own choice, but remember to add 150–200ml (5–7 fl oz) less stock if you are not using the chestnuts.

———— • ————

1 large onion, peeled and chopped
1 tablespoon cooking oil
knob of butter (optional)
4 tablespoons sherry
450g (1lb) Brussels sprouts, trimmed
and quartered

750ml (1½ pints) vegetable stock
175g (6oz) canned chestnuts, drained
(optional)
salt and freshly ground black pepper
4 tablespoons single cream, to serve
(optional)

———— • ————

1. Gently fry the onion in the oil and butter, if using, for 4–5 minutes until the onion starts to soften. Do not allow them to brown.

2. Pour on the sherry and bring to the boil. Add the sprouts, stock, chestnuts if using, and seasoning. Bring to the boil, lower the heat, cover and simmer for about 15 minutes.

3. Purée the soup in a blender or food processor until smooth. Return to the pan and reheat. Serve with a swirl of single cream in each bowl, if liked.

Lettuce and Green Pea Soup with Mint

If, like me, you dislike throwing away food this soup provides a very useful way of using up the tough outside leaves on Cos and Webb lettuces, or indeed any lettuces.

If you do not eat the soup all at one go (or you make double quantity), you can store it in the fridge for two to three days. The flavours will intensify to make an excellent chilled soup to serve when you have even less time to spare.

———————— • ————————

125g (4oz) fresh mint
325g (11oz) outer leaves from a Cos
  or Webb lettuce
225g (8oz) frozen green peas
400g (14oz) potatoes, peeled and finely
  diced

150ml (¼ pint) dry white wine
450ml (¾ pint) water
150ml (5 fl oz) soured cream
salt and freshly ground black pepper

———————— • ————————

1. Strip the mint leaves from the stalks. Chop half the leaves and set aside.

2. Put the lettuce leaves, peas, potatoes, mint stalks and the whole mint leaves in a saucepan with the wine and water. Bring to the boil and simmer for 15 minutes.

3. Purée in a blender with most of the soured cream and seasoning to taste.

4. Pour the soup back into the pan, add the remaining mint and reheat. Serve with a swirl of the remaining soured cream in the centre.

Onion Soup with Toasted Cheese Croûtons

This soup depends for its flavour upon very careful cooking of the onions. Start the onions off on a low heat. Then, once they have softened, turn up the heat to brown them. This way you will get a good flavour without using too much fat.

———— • ————

1kg (2lb) Spanish onions, peeled and
   sliced
1 tablespoon cooking oil
½ teaspoon yeast extract
900ml (1½ pints) boiling water
1 bay leaf
salt and freshly ground black pepper

CROÛTONS
4 large thick slices French bread
125g (4oz) Gruyère or Emmental
   cheese, grated
1 teaspoon Dijon mustard

———— • ————

1. Fry the onions in a large pan in cooking oil until they are all lightly browned.

2. Mix the yeast extract with the boiling water and pour over the onions. Add the bay leaf and seasonings and bring to the boil. Reduce the heat, cover and simmer for 20 minutes.

3. Just before the soup is ready, toast the bread for the croûtons on each side. Mix the cheese and mustard and spread over the toast making sure that it is covering the crusts.

4. Place under the grill and leave until the cheese begins to bubble.

5. Serve the soup in large, shallow soup bowls with a cheese croûton on the top.

Brie and Onion Soup

This creamy soup can be made with any kind of soft cheese, such as Brie or Camembert. Though the cheeses used here are French in origin, the soup actually comes from Germany where many of the creameries now make cheeses which are very similar to their French counterparts. Indeed blue Brie originated in Germany, then the French followed suit.

If you like something that packs a bit more punch, try using a German blue Brie or Cambazola cheese, but remember that the heat will intensify the flavour of the cheese.

—————— • ——————

1 onion, peeled and very finely chopped
40g (1½ oz) butter
25g (1oz) flour
300ml (½ pint) vegetable stock

300ml (½ pint) milk
125g (4oz) Brie with the crust
*   removed*
freshly ground black pepper

—————— • ——————

1. Fry the onion in butter until transparent; do not allow it to brown.

2. Stir in the flour then gradually stir in the stock and milk. Bring to the boil, stirring all the time.

3. Cut the cheese into small pieces and add them to the soup, stirring until they have melted. Season with black pepper and cook for 5 minutes.

Stracciatella with Oyster Mushrooms

'*Stracciatella*' is the classic soup of Latium and the Marches in Central Italy. There it is flavoured with nutmeg and lemon zest respectively both of which are worth trying.

I first thought of adding mushrooms after visiting a mushroom farm in Sussex, and was delighted with the result. Button, shiitake or wild mushrooms will each give you a different flavour.

———— • ————

2 eggs
1 tablespoon fine semolina
2 tablespoons finely grated Parmesan
  cheese, plus extra to serve
1 tablespoon freshly chopped parsley

900ml (1½ pints) good vegetable stock
1 teaspoon yeast extract
75g (3oz) oyster mushrooms, sliced
  thinly

———— • ————

1. Beat the eggs in a bowl with the semolina, Parmesan cheese and parsley. Add about 250ml (8 fl oz) of the vegetable stock and beat to a smooth cream.

2. Mix the yeast extract with a little of the remaining stock. Pour into a pan with the rest of the stock and the mushrooms and bring to the boil. Cook for 1 minute.

3. Pour in the egg and semolina mixture. Beat with a fork for 3–4 minutes until the broth almost returns to the boil and the egg cooks into fine shreds. Serve at once with more cheese.

Curried Cauliflower Soup Ⓥ

Here's a spiced-up version of the French classic cauliflower soup, *Crème Dubarry*. If you have time to make them, it is very good served with fried bread croûtons – to make these, butter both sides of slices of white bread, fry over a medium heat until crisp, then cut into small cubes.

———— • ————

1 tablespoon cooking oil
1 onion, peeled and coarsely chopped
1/2 teaspoon whole cumin seeds
4 tablespoons sherry (optional)
1 medium-sized cauliflower, cut into
    chunks

1/2 teaspoon mild curry powder
700ml (1 1/4 pints) vegetable stock
salt and freshly ground black pepper
3–4 tablespoons single cream, to serve
    (optional)

———— • ————

1. Heat the oil in a saucepan and fry the onion and cumin seeds for 2–3 minutes to soften the onions. Pour on the sherry, if using, and bring to the boil.

2. Add the remaining ingredients except the cream, and bring to the boil again. Cover with a lid, reduce the heat and simmer for 25 minutes.

3. Purée in a blender or food processor, or rub through a sieve. Pour back into the pan and reheat.

4. Swirl cream, if using, into each portion as it is served.

Cauliflower Chowder

A large helping of this vegetable-packed chowder makes a hearty main course. Serve with crusty wholemeal rolls and precede it with an Orange and Mozzarella Salad (page 40) or Horseradish Carrots with Eggs (page 27).

For a change try using broccoli in place of half the cauliflower.

———— • ————

2 onions, peeled and sliced
15g (1/2 oz) butter
1 large cauliflower, broken into florets
450g (1lb) new potatoes, peeled and
  quartered or diced
125g (4oz) frozen peas
125g (4oz) fresh or frozen sweetcorn

900ml (1 1/2 pints) milk
1 bay leaf
pinch dried mixed herbs
salt and freshly ground black pepper
2 tablespoons finely chopped fresh
  parsley

———— • ————

1. Gently fry the onions in butter until transparent then add the remaining ingredients, retaining a little parsley for garnish.

2. Bring to the boil and cover with a lid. Turn the heat down very low and simmer very gently for 15–20 minutes until all the vegetables are tender. Sprinkle with remaining parsley and serve.

Mushroom Soup

Homemade mushroom soup always seems to have so much more flavour than the canned variety, and it is not difficult to make. Use small button mushrooms for a delicately coloured soup, or large field mushrooms for a darker, more robust soup.

———— • ————

15g (1/2 oz) butter
2 teaspoons cooking oil
1 small onion, peeled and sliced
2 medium leeks, washed and sliced
350g (12oz) button mushrooms, wiped and sliced
300ml (1/2 pint) milk
450ml (3/4 pint) vegetable stock

1/4 teaspoon dried oregano
1/4 teaspoon celery salt (optional)
salt and freshly ground black pepper
3 tablespoons single cream or plain yoghurt

GARNISH
1 tablespoon chopped fresh parsley

———— • ————

1. Heat the butter and oil in a large pan and gently fry the onions and leeks for about 2–3 minutes. Take care not to let the vegetables brown.

2. Reserve a few slices of mushroom for garnish. Add the remaining mushrooms, milk, stock, oregano, celery salt, if using, and seasoning to the pan. Bring to the boil, cover and simmer for 20 minutes.

3. Purée in a blender or food processor or rub through a sieve. Return to the pan.

4. Stir the single cream or yoghurt into the soup. Bring to the boil, stirring all the time. Correct the seasoning if necessary.

5. Serve sprinkled with the reserved slices of mushroom and the chopped parsley.

Mint and Cucumber Soup

This idea for a cold soup came from my colleague Pete Smith, the cookery editor of *New Woman* magazine. He spikes his version with Pernod but I prefer the cleaner flavour of fresh herbs on their own. Try it both ways and see what *you* think.

———— • ————

1 large cucumber, roughly chopped
1 clove garlic, peeled and chopped
25g (1oz) fresh mint leaves
8g (¼ oz) fresh parsley sprigs

3 tablespoons mango chutney
salt and freshly ground black pepper
175ml (6 fl oz) soured cream

———— • ————

1. Place all the ingredients except the soured cream in a blender or food processor and blend until smooth.

2. Add the soured cream and blend again. Check the seasoning and correct if necessary.

Chilled Beetroot and Orange Soup

Carrot and orange is a well known combination but orange makes an even better partner for beetroot. The idea originated in Eastern Europe where slightly sweet soups are very popular.

Buy ready-cooked beetroot, but do make sure that it is fresh and has not been dipped in vinegar. It should also be well cooked. If it is underdone it will be difficult to obtain a smooth purée.

———————— • ————————

450g (1lb) well-cooked beetroot, peeled
  and chopped
juice of 2 oranges
grated rind of 1 orange
1 teaspoon ground coriander
450ml (3/4 pint) plain yoghurt

salt and freshly ground black pepper

GARNISH
4 tablespoons plain yoghurt
4 sprigs fresh parsley

———————— • ————————

1. Place all the ingredients in a blender or food processor, retaining a small amount of orange rind for the garnish, and mix to a smooth purée.

2. Chill for 15–20 minutes before serving.

3. Garnish each serving with a swirl of yoghurt, a little of the reserved grated orange rind and a sprig of parsley.

Melon, Ginger and Avocado Soup

This unusual cold soup was inspired by the fruit soups of Hungary. It has a lovely flavour and an interesting slightly grainy, but velvety texture.

———————— • ————————

1 small melon, halved and seeded
1 large ripe avocado, peeled and stoned
juice of 1/2 lemon
150g (5oz) low-fat plain yoghurt

50ml (2 fl oz) skimmed milk
1 teaspoon grated fresh ginger root
salt and freshly ground black pepper

———————— • ————————

1. Reserve 4 thin slices from the melon for garnish. Peel the melon and roughly chop. Place in a blender or food processor with the avocado, lemon and yoghurt.

2. Blend until smooth. Add the milk, ginger and seasoning to taste and blend again.

3. Chill for 15–20 minutes. Serve garnished with the reserved melon slices.

Tomato and Cucumber Soup with Fresh Herbs

Lots of different versions of this soup have appeared on my table since I first tasted it in Sweden. There, dill is the chosen herb but tarragon, basil or chives work just as well.

— • —

600ml (1 pint) tomato juice
1 large orange
150g (5oz) plain yoghurt

5cm (2 inch) piece cucumber, grated
salt and freshly ground black pepper
freshly chopped herbs, to taste

— • —

1. Pour the tomato juice into a bowl and grate in a little of the orange rind.

2. Squeeze the orange and sieve the juice into the bowl. Whisk in the yoghurt and stir in the cucumber. Season to taste.

3. Place in the 'fridge to chill until required. Stir in your chosen herbs just before serving.

· CHAPTER TWO ·

HOT AND COLD STARTERS

WHETHER you need an impressive first course to start a dinner party, or a recipe that can be put together with a minimum of fuss to keep the family happy while you prepare the rest of the meal, you'll find it in this chapter. I have included both hot and cold starters.

Although these recipes are primarily first courses, you could serve some as snacks or salads. The pâtés, for example, can also be used in sandwiches, or to top fingers of toast or croûtons for canapés at a drinks party. The dips, too, are useful for parties, while Guacamole can be used as a dip or a filling for taco shells.

Gratin of Broccoli and Cauliflower with Toasted Almonds

This dish is based on a technique I learnt while on a cookery course at Roger Vergé's school of cookery at his restaurant at the 'Moulin de Mougins' in Provence. It looks and tastes very grand but it really is quite quick and easy to make. Serve as a first course when you are entertaining, or treat yourself to a stunning snack.

———— • ————

1 small cauliflower, divided into florets
1 bunch broccoli
150ml (¼ pint) water
3 egg yolks

250ml (8 fl oz) double cream
salt and freshly ground black pepper
25g (1oz) flaked almonds, toasted

———— • ————

1. Break the cauliflower into florets and cut the stalks off the broccoli. The vegetables should be in fairly small pieces. Place the vegetables in a pan with the water, bring to the boil, cover and simmer for 10 minutes until just tender.

2. Drain the vegetables, retaining the cooking liquor, and arrange in four individual heatproof dishes.

3. Return the cooking liquor to the pan, bring to the boil then simmer for 3–4 minutes. Meanwhile preheat the grill.

4. Mix the egg yolks and cream with the seasoning and stir into the pan of cooking liquor, stirring all the time. Continue heating and stirring until the mixture thickens and starts to coat the back of the spoon. Do not allow the mixture to boil.

5. Pour the sauce over the broccoli and cauliflower and cook under the grill until a light skin forms on the sauce and starts to brown. Sprinkle with toasted almonds.

Artichokes Baked with Goat's Cheese

This recipe is best made with canned artichoke bases rather than artichoke hearts. The latter can be used if you can find any which are not too stringy – in my experience this is difficult!

Any kind of fresh, rindless goat's cheese can be used but I particularly like English Perroche. More economical is the French Roubliac range of goat's cheese. These are available in herb and pepper coated versions, which add extra flavour to the dish. Remember to leave out the ground pepper if you use pepper-coated cheese.

———— • ————

1 × 425g (15oz) can artichoke bases,
  drained and cut in half or quarters
175g (6oz) fresh soft goat's cheese
6 tablespoons plain yoghurt
1 clove of garlic, peeled and crushed

¼ teaspoon dried thyme
freshly ground black pepper
50g (2oz) wholemeal breadcrumbs
2 tablespoons olive oil

———— • ————

1. Preheat the oven to 230°C/450°F/Gas 8. Arrange the artichoke bases in the bottom of an oven-proof dish.

2. Blend the goat's cheese, yoghurt, garlic, thyme and black pepper in a blender or food processor.

3. Spread the mixture over the artichokes and top with breadcrumbs. Drizzle with olive oil and bake for 10–15 minutes until the breadcrumbs are brown.

Cheese and Prune Purses

These parcels make a wonderful starter for a light meal. They may seem a little fiddly to make but I can do it in about 10–15 minutes while the oven is heating up. They then take about 10 minutes to cook – just time to prepare a main course salad.

———— • ————

125g (4oz) Saint Agur cheese, chopped
50g (2oz) curd cheese
24 large French prunes, stoned

12 walnut halves
12 × 15cm (6 inch) squares filo pastry
melted butter

———— • ————

1. Set the oven to 200°C/400°F/Gas 6.

2. Mix the two cheeses together with a fork and use the mixture to sandwich the prunes together in pairs, adding a walnut half in the centre of each one.

3. Brush the pastry squares with melted butter and place a double prune in the centre.

4. Gather up the edges of the pastry over the prunes and twist lightly to form purses.

5. Place on a tray and bake for about 10 minutes until crisp and golden.

Egg Pots Provençale

You can just about get this dish, inspired by the wonderful vegetable dishes of Provence, prepared and cooked in half an hour. Serve with melba toast and start the meal with a French onion soup. Follow with Egyptian Rice (page 153).

———————— • ————————

1 small onion, peeled and chopped
2 tablespoons olive oil
1 small aubergine, diced
1 courgette, diced
1 small green pepper, seeded and diced
1 small red pepper, seeded and diced
4 tomatoes, chopped

1 tablespoon tomato purée
2 tablespoons water
salt and freshly ground black pepper
4 eggs
4 tablespoons single cream
1 tablespoon freshly grated Parmesan cheese

———————— • ————————

1. Set the oven to 200°C/400°F/Gas 6.

2. Gently fry the onions in the oil for 2 minutes. Add all the vegetables and fry for a further 2 minutes. Mix the tomato purée with the water and seasoning and pour over the vegetables. Cover and cook over a low heat for 10 minutes.

3. Divide the mixture between four large ramekin dishes. Make a well in the centre and break an egg into each one. Top with cream and cheese.

4. Place on a baking sheet and bake for 10–12 minutes until the egg white has set but the yolk is still runny. Serve at once.

Opposite: Orange and Mozzarella Salad with Chervil (page 40) and Tuscan Chickpea Soup with Pasta (page 10)

Horseradish Carrots with Eggs

This simple mix of ingredients gives a wonderfully delicate balance of flavours. Follow with a thick soup like Cauliflower Chowder or Grilled Mushrooms and Pesto Sauce, and rice (pages 17 and 107).

———— • ————

*350g (12oz) carrots, peeled and very
    coarsely grated
1 small onion, peeled and grated
2 tablespoons cooking oil*

*3 teaspoons creamed horseradish
salt and freshly ground black pepper
4 eggs*

———— • ————

1. Preheat the oven to 200°C/400°F/Gas 6. Grease four individual ramekin dishes.

2. Stir-fry the vegetables in the oil for 3–4 minutes until they start to soften. Stir in the horseradish thoroughly, add the seasoning and transfer to the ramekins.

3. Break an egg into each ramekin and bake for 15–20 minutes until the eggs are set to your liking.

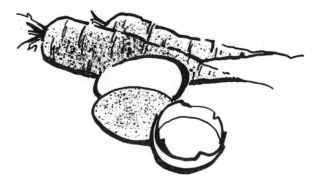

Opposite: Egg Pots Provençale (page 26)

Stuffed Red Peppers Ⓥ

If I have time I like to make double quantity of these delicately flavoured stuffed peppers. One batch is served as soon as it is cooked, while the other is left to cool and kept in the 'fridge for a day or so to be eaten cold with a good olive-oil-based vinaigrette.

———— • ————

1 small onion, peeled and chopped
½ small green pepper, seeded and
  chopped
2 tablespoons olive oil
½ teaspoon paprika

50g (2oz) fresh or frozen peas
75g (3oz) rice
200ml (7 fl oz) vegetable stock
salt and freshly ground black pepper
4 small red peppers

———— • ————

1. Gently fry the onion and green pepper in 1 tablespoon of the oil until tender. Stir in the paprika, making sure it doesn't burn, and add the peas.

2. Stir in the rice and add the remaining oil, the stock and seasoning. Bring to the boil, then stir again and reduce the heat and cook for 15 minutes until the rice is tender and the liquid absorbed.

3. Meanwhile, preheat the grill. Grill the red peppers for 4–5 minutes, turning once or twice until well-charred and beginning to soften.

4. When the peppers are cool enough to handle, cut off the tops. Scoop out the seeds and fill with the cooked rice mixture.

5. Return to the grill for about 5 minutes to warm through.

Tomatoes Stuffed with Shiitake Mushrooms Ⓥ

I first tried this recipe with shiitake mushrooms and I was very pleased with their delicate flavour. However, ordinary mushrooms can also be used.

———— • ————

8 large tomatoes, with the tops cut off
salt and freshly ground black pepper
4 tablespoons cooking oil
350g (12oz) shiitake mushrooms,
    sliced
2 teaspoons finely chopped tarragon, or
    ½ teaspoon dried tarragon

1 teaspoon freshly chopped thyme, or
    ¼ teaspoon dried thyme
a little grated lemon rind
125ml (4 fl oz) vegetable stock or dry
    white wine
broadleaf parsley, for garnish

———— • ————

1. Preheat the grill. Scoop the seeds and centres out of the tomatoes and discard. Season the tomatoes and place under the grill for 2–3 minutes to heat through.

2. Meanwhile, heat the oil in a frying pan and add the remaining ingredients except the stock and parsley. Stir-fry over a medium heat for 2–3 minutes.

3. Add the stock to the pan and boil rapidly over a high heat until reduced and thickened.

4. Spoon the mushroom mixture into the hot tomatoes and serve at once garnished with broadleaf parsley.

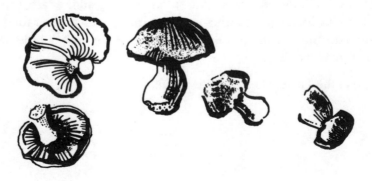

Cauliflower with Guacamole Ⓥ

Guacamole is one of the most versatile sauces I know. In this dish I have teamed it with lightly-cooked cauliflower and the result is stunning. Cooked beetroot makes a fitting accompaniment. Guacamole can be more traditionally served with taco shells or with fresh vegetable crudités and corn chips.

———— • ————

1 cauliflower, trimmed
2 tablespoons olive oil
1 tablespoon wine vinegar
salt and freshly ground black pepper

juice of 1 lemon
1 tablespoon finely chopped onion
salt and freshly ground black pepper
1 large ripe avocado

GUACAMOLE
1 ripe tomato
3–4 sprigs fresh coriander

———— • ————

1. Steam the cauliflower in a little salted boiling water, in a covered saucepan, for about 10–15 minutes until just tender. It should not be mushy but retain a little bite to it. Drain and plunge into cold water to cool.

2. Meanwhile, finely chop the tomato and coriander for the Guacamole.

3. Break the cauliflower into florets and place in a bowl. Toss in the oil and vinegar and season to taste.

4. Mix half the lemon juice for the Guacamole in a bowl with the tomato, coriander, onion and seasoning.

5. At the last moment, peel and stone the avocado. Mash the flesh and remaining lemon juice with a fork or purée in a blender or food processor. Stir into the tomato and onion mixture. Thin with a little water if the mixture is too thick.

6. Spoon the Guacamole over the cauliflower.

Eggs with Salsa Verde

In Italy, *salsa verde* is served with all kinds of cold foods and salads. It is also good poured over warm new potatoes, or mixed baby vegetables instead of eggs but remember that you will still only need one hard-boiled egg.

———— • ————

½ slice day-old white bread with crusts removed, broken into pieces
1 tablespoon white wine or cider vinegar
5 hard-boiled eggs
2 tablespoons freshly chopped parsley

2 tablespoons freshly chopped basil
1 teaspoon freshly chopped mint
1 teaspoon capers, chopped
3 tablespoons olive oil
water or lemon juice
sprigs of fresh herbs for garnish

———— • ————

1. Soak the bread in the vinegar for 5 minutes.

2. Meanwhile, peel one of the eggs and rub the yolk through a sieve. Chop the egg white and save to use as a garnish with the fresh herbs.

3. Mash the soaked bread, then add the herbs, capers and sieved egg yolk and mix together.

4. Gradually stir in the oil, beating well with a fork until the mixture has a sauce-like consistency. If the mixture is too thick add a little water or lemon juice.

5. Peel the remaining eggs and cut in half. Place, cut-side down, on a large plate, or individual plates and pour the sauce over the top.

Avocado with Walnuts and
Raspberry Vinegar Ⓥ

Walnut oil is a relative newcomer to the kitchen and so there are no long-standing traditions for its use. I came across the combination of walnut oil and avocado quite by accident but the marriage is an inspired one.

Avocado is an oily fruit and olive oil dressings only seem to over-emphasise this. Walnut oil, however, has a slightly bitter note which complements the avocado's creaminess. I have added raspberry vinegar for flavour, and chopped walnuts for interest and texture.

———— • ————

50g (2oz) walnut halves
2 large ripe avocados

DRESSING
8 tablespoons walnut oil
1½ tablespoons raspberry vinegar
salt and freshly ground black pepper

GARNISH
sprigs of fresh parsley or chervil
fresh raspberries

———— • ————

1. Coarsely chop half of the walnuts. Mix the dressing ingredients and stir in the chopped walnuts. Leave to stand until required.

2. Halve, stone and peel the avocados. Slice each half lengthways several times then spread out the slices in a fan shape.

3. Arrange on four serving plates and dot with the remaining walnuts. Spoon the dressing over the top, garnish with sprigs of parsley or chervil and raspberries and serve immediately.

Tropical Fruit Cocktail

I was lucky enough to go to the Colony Club Hotel in Barbados last year and this was a popular first course. The only difference is that the herbs used there are more likely to be spring onions or parsley. My version, with coriander, packs more of a punch.

———— • ————

1 ripe avocado
juice of ½ lemon
1 ripe papaya (pawpaw)
juice of ½ lime

¼ teaspoon cayenne pepper
3 tablespoons coarsely chopped fresh
   coriander leaves
3 tablespoons plain yoghurt

———— • ————

1. Peel, stone and chop the avocado and immediately mix it with the lemon juice to stop it discolouring.

2. Peel the papaya and remove the seeds. Cut into the same size pieces as the avocado.

3. Mix the papaya and avocado with the remaining ingredients and serve at once.

Avocado Stuffed Tomatoes

Avocados are one of my favourite foods and I usually have one or two ripening on my fruit bowl. This mixture of avocado and Greek yoghurt is very versatile. As well as using it to fill tomatoes, I stuff sticks of celery or fill baby taco shells with it.

————— • —————

4 medium-to-large tomatoes
1 large ripe avocado
juice and grated rind of 1 lemon
2 spring onions, very finely chopped

1 teaspoon grated fresh ginger
150g (5oz) Greek yoghurt
salt and freshly ground black pepper

————— • —————

1. Cut the tomatoes in half. Scoop out the seeds and centres and discard. Season lightly and keep on one side.

2. Peel and stone the avocado and mix the flesh immediately with the lemon juice to prevent discolouration. Rub the mixture through a sieve or process in a blender or food processor.

3. Stir or mix in the lemon rind, spring onions and ginger. Next fold in the yoghurt, season to taste and use to fill the prepared tomatoes.

Goat's Cheese and Watercress Pâté

There is no reason why vegetarians should not enjoy a good pâté. This one, made with a semi-soft goat's cheese such as a chevre log, has a really tangy flavour, but if you prefer a lighter flavour use milder Chabi or St Maure. Serve with fingers of toast or strips of baked pitta bread (see page 43).

————— • —————

1 bunch watercress, trimmed and
chopped
125g (4oz) goat's cheese, chopped
5 spring onions, trimmed and finely
chopped

3 tablespoons quark or fromage frais
freshly ground black pepper

1. Place all the ingredients in a bowl and mix well with a fork.

2. Spoon into a dish or bowl and serve with toast or strips of baked pitta bread.

Tofu and Watercress Pâté ⓥ

This recipe started off as a simple vegan alternative to the previous recipe for Goat's Cheese and Watercress Pâté, but it grew into a full blown recipe in its own right. It is light and fresh, and very good served with wheat crackers or rye crispbread.

———— • ————

1 bunch watercress, trimmed and
*   chopped*
175g (6oz) tofu
50g (2oz) ground almonds
4 spring onions, trimmed and finely
*   chopped*

2 tablespoons freshly chopped parsley
a little grated lemon rind
salt and freshly ground black pepper

———— • ————

1. Place all the ingredients in a bowl and mix well with a fork.

2. Spoon into a dish or bowl and serve with wheat crackers or rye crispbread.

Three-Fruit Salad Ⓥ

Fruit salad is usually thought of as a dessert, but this mixture makes an excellent first course. Balsamic vinegar is a special vinegar from Modena in Italy. It is made from grape must rather than wine, and is aged for a long time. There are lots of imitations, so buy the best you can afford. You do not need to use very much at one time, so it will last a long while. Avoid the cheaper stuff (under £5) as it is just flavoured caramel.

———————— • ————————

2 kiwifruit, peeled and sliced
2 Sharon fruit, sliced
2 large tomatoes, sliced
small amount of mixed salad leaves
2 tablespoons toasted pine nuts
2 tablespoons black olives
sprigs of fresh parsley

DRESSING
6 tablespoons extra virgin olive oil
1/4–1/2 teaspoon good quality balsamic
  vinegar
salt and freshly ground black pepper

———————— • ————————

1. Arrange the slices from the three fruits in an overlapping rosette on each plate.

2. Place a few mixed leaves on the side and dot with black olives and sprigs of parsley.

3. Mix the dressing ingredients and sprinkled over.

Red Pepper Salad Ⓥ

This deceptively simple salad is from the La Mancha region of Central Spain. Grilling the vegetables adds a delicious smoky flavour.

When you have time, make double the quantity and leave half in the refrigerator for a day or two; the flavour will then be even better.

———————— • ————————

4 large red peppers, cut in half and
   seeded
1 large ripe continental tomato
4 large cloves garlic, with skins on

4 tablespoons freshly chopped parsley
4 tablespoons extra virgin olive oil
1 teaspoon wine vinegar
salt and freshly ground black pepper

———————— • ————————

1. Preheat the grill. Grill the peppers, garlic and tomato until lightly charred. Leave the peppers to cool slightly then, working over a bowl to catch the juices, peel them and cut into strips. Peel the tomato.

2. Make the dressing. Peel and crush the garlic and mix with half the parsley, the peeled tomato and salt using a mortar and pestle or a blender. Then add the oil, any juice from the peppers, and the vinegar.

3. Arrange the pepper strips in a serving dish and pour the dressing over the top. Sprinkle with the remaining chopped parsley. This salad will keep several days in the 'fridge.

4. Serve with really good bread to mop up the dressing.

———————————— 37 ————————————

Mushroom Salad with Fennel Ⓥ

Mushrooms and fennel are two of my favourite vegetables and as their flavours really blend well together I could not resist using them to make this well textured salad. Serve on a bed of lettuce with crusty brown rolls.

———— • ————

175g (6oz) button mushrooms, sliced
3 tablespoons olive or salad oil
1 tablespoon lemon juice
2 bulbs fennel, quartered

salt and freshly ground black pepper
½ teaspoon ground coriander
2 tablespoons freshly chopped parsley

———— • ————

1. Mix the mushrooms with the oil and lemon juice and leave to stand while preparing the rest of the recipe.

2. Cook the fennel in lightly salted water for 5 minutes or until fairly firm, but no longer hard. Drain and plunge into cold water.

3. Drain the fennel again and chop finely. Stir into the mushrooms with the coriander, parsley and black pepper.

4. Chill for a few minutes or until required.

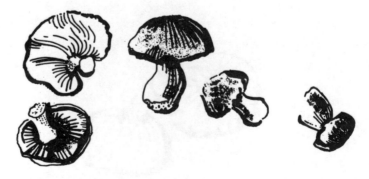

Chicory and Carrot Salad with
Oyster Mushrooms ⓥ

I serve this simple gourmet treat at the start of a special meal. It is very quick to make and leaves plently of time to prepare the rest of the meal. Follow it with Glazed Garlic Tofu and Braised Spicy Aubergines with rice (pages 86 and 124).

―――――― • ――――――

125g (4oz) oyster mushrooms, cut into
  large chunks
2 tablespoons light soy sauce
1/2 teaspoon orange rind
150ml (5 fl oz) orange juice
pinch five spice powder
2 heads of chicory finely sliced

2 carrots, peeled and grated
2 tablespoons salad oil
1 teaspoon sesame oil

GARNISH
orange segments
fresh coriander or Continental parsley

―――――― • ――――――

1. Put the mushrooms into a saucepan with the soy sauce, orange rind and juice and five spice powder. Bring to the boil and simmer for 1–2 minutes, until the mushrooms are cooked. Keep on one side.

2. Mix the chicory with the carrots and oils.

3. Press the salad mixture into four ramekin dishes and carefully turn out on to four individual plates.

4. Drain the mushrooms and put on top of the unmoulded salads. Garnish with orange segments and coriander or parsley leaves.

Orange and Mozzarella Salad with Chervil

If possible use traditional buffalo milk mozzarella as it has much more flavour and a better texture than the more usual cow's milk variety. Please avoid Danish block-shaped mozzarella as it is tasteless and rubbery. Served with a large piece of Italian bread this salad also makes a substantial snack.

———— • ————

4 oranges, peeled and sliced
2 × 200g (7oz) mozzarella cheeses, sliced

DRESSING
6 tablespoons extra virgin olive oil
1 tablespoon wine or cider vinegar
2 tablespoons freshly chopped chervil

pinch mixed dried herbs
salt and freshly ground black pepper

GARNISH
sprigs of chervil
stoned black olives, cut in half or into quarters

———— • ————

1. Arrange the slices of orange and mozzarella in an attractive pattern on four individual plates.

2. Mix the dressing ingredients and pour over the salads.

3. Garnish with sprigs of chervil and olives.

Avocado Salad with Hot Grapefruit Sauce

Grapefruit and avocado is a tried and tested combination in my kitchen, but I wanted to use something a little more adventurous than simple grapefruit segments. The result was this deliciously rich sauce which really matches the velvety texture of avocados.

———— • ————

125g (4oz) mixed salad leaves such as curly endive, chicory and lettuce
4 large ripe tomatoes, peeled, seeded and finely chopped
3 grapefruit

2 ripe avocados
1 box of salad cress
75g (3oz) unsalted butter, cut into small pieces

1. Arrange the salad leaves attractively on four individual plates. Place the tomatoes in a sieve to drain.

2. Squeeze the grapefruit and strain the juice into a saucepan. Bring to the boil and boil rapidly until reduced to about 4 tablespoons.

3. Meanwhile, halve, peel and stone the avocados. Slice each half lengthways several times then spread out to make a fan shape. Arrange on the salad leaves. Place mounds of tomato and cress on the salad.

4. Whisk the butter, a piece at a time, into the grapefruit juice until the mixture thickens. Do not allow to boil. Pour over the avocados and serve at once.

Lettuce Parcels with Italian Pecorino and Walnut Salad

I first had this cheese and walnut mixture in the hill town of San Gimignano in Tuscany when it was served as a topping for crostini. I still serve it in that way for parties, but I have found that it also makes a very good starter when served in a well-flavoured lettuce such as Webbs, lollo rosso or oak leaf.

———— • ————

125g (4oz) Pecorino cheese, diced
50g (2oz) walnut halves, coarsely
    chopped
4 tablespoons freshly chopped parsley
4 tablespoons olive oil
1 tablespoon garlic-flavoured wine
    vinegar
1 clove garlic, crushed

freshly ground black pepper
1/2 well-flavoured lettuce such as
    Webbs Wonder, lollo rosso or
    oak leaf

GARNISH
6–8 cherry tomatoes
sprigs of Continental parsley

———— • ————

1. Place all the ingredients, except the lettuce leaves, in a bowl and mix well together.

2. Spoon the mixture on to the lettuce leaves and roll up into parcels. Garnish with cherry tomatoes and sprigs of parsley.

Curried Chestnut Dip with Crudités

This is an extremely quick recipe to make. Be sure to use the unsweetened canned chestnuts or you could end up with a very odd dip indeed!

———— • ————

1 × 225g (8oz) can unsweetened
whole chestnuts
225g (8oz) quark or low-fat soft cheese
1 heaped teaspoon curry powder
salt and freshly ground black pepper

CRUDITÉS
4 sticks celery, cut into small sticks
10cm (4 inch) piece cucumber, cut into
sticks
1 large carrot, peeled and cut into
sticks

———— • ————

1. Drain the chestnuts and reserve 2 tablespoons of the liquid. Purée the chestnuts or rub through a sieve.

2. Turn the purée into a bowl and gradually add the quark or soft cheese, beating well with a wooden spoon to ensure a really smooth consistency. Thin with the reserved chestnut liquid and stir in the curry powder and seasonings.

3. Spoon into four small ramekin dishes and serve with the crudités arranged around the outside.

Lebanese Cheese Dip with Baked Pitta Bread

The recipe for this dip comes from my local Lebanese restaurant but the idea of baking the pitta bread strips is my own.

———— • ————

4 pitta bread
2 tablespoons olive oil
3 tablespoons sesame seeds

LEBANESE CHEESE DIP
225g (8oz) feta cheese
1 tablespoon water
juice of 1 lemon
2 tablespoons olive oil

1 Italian, red or mild onion, peeled
  and finely chopped
½ large cucumber, peeled and diced

GARNISH
sprigs of fresh parsley
slices of cucumber
black olives

———— • ————

1. Preheat the oven to 200°C/400°F/Gas 6.

2. Brush the pitta bread all over with olive oil. Cut into long thin strips. Place on a baking sheet and sprinkle with sesame seeds. Bake for 5–6 minutes until crisp and golden.

3. Meanwhile make the dip. Mash the cheese in the water using a fork. Then add the lemon juice followed by the oil, still mixing with a fork. Finally mix in the onion and cucumber. The result should still be quite chunky – almost like oily cottage cheese.

4. Spoon the mixture into a bowl and garnish with parsley, cucumber slices and olives. Serve with the freshly baked pitta bread strips.

Chicory Spears with Cucumber Hummus

This is a quick and easy dish to make to hand round with a glass of wine or an aperitif in lieu of the first course. Follow it with Spaghetti with Sunflower Seeds and Sun-dried Tomatoes, or Broad Bean and Okra Couscous (pages 137 and 164).

———— • ————

300g (10oz) ready-made hummus
175g (6oz) plain yoghurt
juice of 1 lemon
15cm (6 inch) piece cucumber, finely diced

50g (2oz) bunch mint, freshly chopped
salt and freshly ground black pepper
4 heads of chicory, separated into spears

———— • ————

1. Mix together the hummus, yoghurt and lemon juice to give a good thick consistency.

2. Stir in the cucumber and mint. Season to taste.

3. Arrange the chicory spears on a plate and place a heaped teaspoonful of the cucumber hummus on each one.

Chicory Spears with Orange Spiced Tabbouleh Ⓥ

Here is a totally different variation on the same theme as Chicory Spears with Cucumber Hummus. It takes just a little longer to prepare but it makes a very good starter. Both recipes make good finger food to serve with drinks and they are always popular.

———— • ————

75g (3oz) bulgar
4 tablespoons freshly chopped parsley
grated rind of 1 orange
1/4 small red pepper, seeded and very finely chopped
2 1/2 tablespoons olive oil
2 tablespoons lemon juice
1/4 teaspoon ground cinnamon

1/4 teaspoon ground coriander
salt and freshly ground black pepper
3–4 heads chicory, separated into spears

GARNISH
4 or 5 mandarin orange segments

———— • ————

1. Place the bulgar in a bowl and cover with plenty of water. Leave to stand for 20 minutes.

2. Drain very well, squeezing out all the water with your fingers. Mix with the remaining ingredients except the chicory and orange segments.

3. Arrange the chicory spears on a large serving plate. Place a spoonful of the bulgar mixture on each spear of chicory.

4. Garnish with mandarin orange segments.

· CHAPTER THREE ·

SNACKS

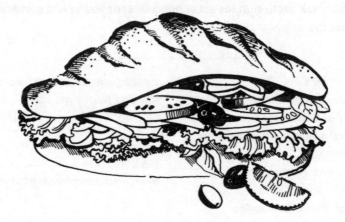

THE RECIPES in this chapter are mostly even faster to prepare than those in the others. They are designed for the occasions when all you have time for is a quick dash to the store cupboard or 'fridge and the bare minimum of preparation and cooking. The dishes are both filling and nutritious so do not need any accompaniments.

Bread is the basic ingredient of many of these snacks. It is used either for sandwiches or is toasted to make a base for a variety of toppings. These range from the traditional classic Welsh Rarebit from the UK to variations on Italian *bruschetta* (ciabatta bread topped with olive oil and garlic and sometimes with chopped tomatoes and basil).

Some of the cold snacks, like Double Decker Sandwiches, Cheese and Carrot Muffins and Pan Bagnat, can be made in advance for desk or school lunches or for picnics.

The spiced filling for the tostados (page 59) takes about half an hour to make, but if you prepare a large batch when you have time, and store it in the 'fridge or freezer, the dish will be ready in the time it takes to warm the tostados in the oven.

Peanut Pâté Double Deckers

I am a peanut butter fan and am happy to eat it in all kinds of ways. Watercress and beetroot are my favourite accompaniments, but I have one American friend who loves peanut butter with cranberry sauce and another who goes for sweet and sour gherkins. You probably have your own favourites.

The pâté makes enough for six sandwiches, or you could serve it with toast or pitta fingers.

———— • ————

PEANUT PÂTÉ
3 tablespoons peanut butter
125g (4oz) soft cheese or drained tofu
2 cloves garlic, peeled and finely
  chopped
2 tablespoons plain yoghurt or soured
  cream
a few drops of Tabasco sauce

freshly ground black pepper

DOUBLE DECKERS
slices of wholemeal bread
slices of pumpernickel (optional)
butter or mayonnaise for spreading
shredded lettuce
chopped watercress or sliced beetroot

———— • ————

1. Place the peanut butter and cheese or drained tofu in a bowl and blend well with a fork.

2. Mix in the remaining ingredients. Store in the refrigerator.

3. To make the double deckers, butter 2 slices of wholemeal bread and 1 of pumpernickel bread, or 3 slices of wholemeal bread per double decker. Alternatively spread the bread with a little mayonnaise.

4. Spread peanut pâté over 1 slice of wholemeal bread. Top with pumpernickel bread or another slice of wholemeal bread.

5. Arrange the lettuce and watercress or beetroot on top then cover with another slice of wholemeal bread. Cut into 4 triangles to serve.

Liptauer Cheese

This is a wonderfully rich concoction from old world Hungary. Friends in Budapest press it into a small pudding basin to turn out and slice. It is delicious eaten in the traditional way with home-baked rye bread and celery, but it can also be used in rye deckers with sweet and sour cucumbers. Alternatively serve with Hungarian Salad (page 74) and lettuce leaves.

———— • ————

175g (6oz) soft cheese
125g (4oz) butter, well softened
1 heaped teaspoon paprika pepper
1/2 teaspoon French mustard

1 tablespoon capers, chopped
1 tablespoon freshly chopped chives
salt and freshly ground black pepper

———— • ————

1. Beat the cheese and butter together with a wooden spoon until they are very well mixed.

2. Beat in the remaining ingredients and spoon into a small pudding basin or large ramekin dish.

3. Place in the 'fridge to chill until required. If you are in a hurry pop it in the freezer for 10 minutes, but don't forget it.

4. Unmould the cheese and cut into wedges to serve.

Cheese and Carrot Muffins

Why is it that modern versions of the food we grew up with never seem to taste the same? I find this with muffins. They are never quite chewy enough nowadays! Nevertheless, they do make a change from ordinary rolls and baps.

Here is one of my favourite recipes from childhood picnics at Southport or New Brighton.

225g (8oz) mature Cheddar cheese,
   grated
1 medium sized carrot, peeled and
   grated

1/4 bunch watercress, coarsely chopped
salt and freshly ground black pepper
25g (1oz) butter, well softened
4 muffins, split open

————— • —————

1. Mix the cheese, carrot, watercress and seasoning in a bowl and add butter to bind the mixture together.

2. Fill the muffins. Wrap in cling film until required.

Anglo-French Baguette

The ex-Lancashire town of Stalybridge (it's in Cheshire now but still looks like a Lancashire mill town) is twinned with the French town of Armentière and this recipe celebrates the connection.

————— • —————

1 × 20cm (8 inch) French loaf
   (baguette)
225g (8oz) Lancashire cheese, grated
1 hard-boiled egg, peeled and chopped
4 cocktail gherkins, chopped
4 stuffed olives, chopped

1 teaspoon freshly chopped chives
1/2 teaspoon French mustard
2 tablespoons mayonnaise
salt and freshly ground black pepper
lettuce leaves

————— • —————

1. Cut the French loaf in half lengthways and hollow out a little by removing some of the dough.

2. Place the remaining ingredients except the lettuce in a bowl and mix together well with a fork.

3. Line both pieces of French loaf with lettuce leaves. Spread the cheese mixture along the length of the base and cover with the lettuce-lined top.

4. Squeeze together with your hands. Slice into 2.5cm/1 inch lengths to serve.

Avocado, Tomato and Fresh Coriander Rolls Ⓥ

This filling is rather like a chunky version of Guacamole. It makes a really good snack served on wholemeal rolls or French bread. I also like it served in taco shells which have been warmed in the oven.

———— • ————

1 ripe avocado
2 tomatoes, peeled, seeded and diced
5 small spring onions (25g/1oz),
   trimmed and finely chopped
1 clove garlic, peeled and crushed
bunch of coriander (about 75g/3oz),
   freshly chopped

juice of 1 lemon
salt and freshly ground black pepper
4 wholemeal rolls

GARNISH
8 large sprigs of parsley

———— • ————

1. Mix together all ingredients, except the rolls, in a bowl.

2. Cut the rolls in half and take out a little of the soft centre.

3. Pile the avocado mixture on to each half and garnish with sprigs of parsley.

Classic Welsh Rarebit

This is such a delicious Welsh rarebit that I can eat two rounds at a sitting! However, this quantity will serve four people for a quick snack.

———— • ————

25g (1oz) butter or margarine
25g (1oz) flour
250ml (8 fl oz) beer
125ml (4 fl oz) skimmed milk
125g (4oz) grated Cheddar cheese
½–1 teaspoon prepared English
   mustard

cayenne pepper
4 large slices wholemeal bread

OPTIONAL FLAVOURINGS
1 tablespoon capers, chopped
1 tablespoon gherkins, chopped
1 tablespoon walnuts, chopped

———— • ————

1. Preheat the grill. Place the butter or margarine, the flour, beer and milk in a saucepan. Bring to the boil over a low heat, whisking all the time with a wire whisk.

2. Toast the bread. Turn the grill to medium hot.

3. When the mixture boils and thickens, cook for a further minute. Stir in the mustard, cayenne pepper to taste and any or all of the optional flavourings.

4. Spread the bread generously with the cheese mixture. Grill for 4–5 minutes until brown.

Extra-Quick Welsh Rarebit

This is an even quicker version of Welsh rarebit than the Classic recipe on page 50. The topping cooks in the time it takes to make the toast.

———— • ————

4 slices wholemeal bread
225g (8oz) Cheddar cheese, grated
50g (2oz) butter

4 tablespoons brown ale or beer
salt
cayenne pepper

———— • ————

1. Preheat the grill. Toast the bread. Place on a plate.

2. Meanwhile, place the remaining ingredients in a pan and stir over a medium heat until all the ingredients have melted.

3. Pour the cheese mixture over the prepared toast. Put under a hot grill for a couple of minutes before serving.

Oriental Cheese Toasts

Very often the simplest foods are the tastiest and this is certainly true of this lightly curried version of cheese on toast. Any kind of chutney can be used, so vary the flavour by experimenting with different types.

———— • ————

125g (4oz) Cheddar cheese, grated
2 tablespoons ginger chutney
1 teaspoon mild curry powder

4 large slices wholemeal bread
4 tomatoes, sliced

———— • ————

1. Preheat the grill. Mix the cheese, chutney and curry powder to a thick paste.

2. Toast the bread then top each slice with tomatoes. Spread the cheese mixture over the top and grill for 3–4 minutes until the cheese is bubbly.

Cheese and Salsa Toasts

I love cheese on toast in any shape or form. This version uses a Mexican-style salsa to give a spicy finish, making a change from the more usual Worcestershire (usually non-veggie!) sauce.

If you have time, make a double quantity of the salsa and store in the 'fridge to use with tacos or grilled vegetables.

———— • ————

4 thick slices country bread, or Italian
　ciabatta loaf or a 20–22.5cm (8–
　9 inch) French loaf cut open
　lengthwise
4 tablespoons extra virgin olive oil
175g (6oz) mature Cheddar cheese,
　grated

SALSA
2 tomatoes, peeled and finely chopped

1 green chilli pepper, seeded and
　chopped
1/2 bunch spring onions, trimmed and
　finely chopped
1/2 small pickled cucumber, finely
　chopped
1 clove garlic, peeled and finely
　chopped (optional)
3 tablespoons freshly chopped parsley,
　basil, coriander or tarragon

———— • ————

1. Preheat the grill. Mix all the ingredients for the salsa in a bowl.

2. Brush both sides of each slice of bread with a little olive oil and toast on each side.

3. Spread the cheese over the toast, taking it to the edge of the bread. Spoon the salsa down the middle.

4. Return to the grill and serve as soon as the cheese starts to bubble.

Egg and Courgette Bake

This all-in-one dish only needs the addition of buttered potatoes or crusty rolls. It is really quick to prepare and looks after itself once it goes in the oven, leaving you free to do your exercises or read a book! Start the meal with a simple tomato salad with a yoghurt and fresh herb dressing.

———— • ————

225g (8oz) courgettes, diced
25g (1oz) butter
small clove garlic, peeled and crushed
6 spring onions, trimmed and chopped
400g (14oz) can butter beans

5 eggs
4 tablespoons milk
75g (3oz) Cheddar cheese
salt and pepper

———— • ————

1. Set the oven to 180°C/350°F/Gas 4.

2. Gently fry the courgettes in the butter for 2–3 minutes until they begin to soften. Add the garlic and spring onion and cook for another two minutes. Stir in the butter beans and transfer to an ovenproof pie dish.

3. Beat the eggs and milk together and stir in the cheese and seasoning. Pour this mixture over the vegetables. Bake in the oven for about 20 minutes until puffed up and golden.

Mushroom Bruschetta ⓥ

With the spread in the popularity of Mediterranean-style food, chefs and cooks have felt free to add all kinds of different toppings to ciabatta bread to make creative variations of *bruschetta*. Here is one of my favourites. It has been Anglicised slightly by using English field mushrooms rather than the much more expensive Italian *porcini*.

———— • ————

2 cloves garlic, peeled and crushed
6 tablespoons extra virgin olive oil
8 large field mushrooms
salt and freshly ground black pepper
4 tablespoons white wine

1 Italian ciabatta loaf, sliced
 lengthways and cut into two
2 tomatoes, peeled, seeded and chopped
2 tablespoons freshly chopped parsley
2 tablespoons freshly chopped spring
 onion

———— • ————

1. Preheat the grill. Mix the garlic and olive oil and use 3–4 tablespoons to brush the gills of the field mushrooms. Sprinkle with salt and place on a grill tray. Sprinkle on the white wine and grill for 4–5 minutes until cooked through. Remove from the grill.

2. Meanwhile, brush the remaining garlic oil over the pieces of ciabatta bread.

3. Toast the bread.

4. Arrange the mushrooms on the toasted ciabatta. Mix the tomato, parsley, spring onion and seasoning. Sprinkle over the top and place under the grill for a further 1–2 minutes. Serve at once.

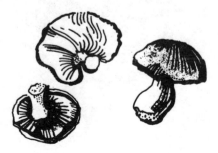

Aubergine Bruschetta with Coriander and Sesame Ⓥ

This is another of the many variations of simple Italian *bruschetta* which I dream up almost every week. Each one is a little different, but extra virgin olive oil and garlic remain constant!

———————— • ————————

6 tablespoons extra virgin olive oil
2 cloves garlic, peeled and chopped
1 teaspoon sesame oil
4 tablespoons freshly chopped coriander

2 small aubergines, trimmed and sliced
   lengthways into 8 slices
1 Italian ciabatta loaf, cut lengthways
   and then cut into two pieces
2 teaspoons toasted sesame seeds

———————— • ————————

1. Preheat the grill. Mix the oil, garlic, sesame oil and 1 tablespoon of chopped coriander. Brush about half the mixture over the slices of aubergine.

2. Arrange on the grill rack and grill on each side for about 10 minutes until browned and cooked through. Keep warm.

3. Brush each piece of ciabatta with the remaining oil and garlic mixture and toast on both sides.

4. Place the aubergines on the toasted bread and sprinkle over the toasted sesame seeds and the rest of the coriander.

Aubergine and Mozzarella Bruschetta

I'm so fond of aubergines that I offer no apology for including another type of aubergine *bruschetta*!

——— • ———

450g (1lb) aubergines, trimmed
1 Italian ciabatta loaf, cut in half
   lengthways then cut into two pieces
1 clove garlic, halved
2 tablespoons olive oil

2 tablespoons tomato purée
14 leaves fresh basil
1 × 200g (7oz) buffalo mozzarella
   cheese, sliced
salt and freshly ground black pepper

——— • ———

1. Preheat the grill. Slice the aubergines and grill on both sides until cooked through and golden. Cut off the skins, if liked.

2. Toast the ciabatta on the underside. Remove from grill – leave the grill on.

3. Rub the cut surfaces of ciabatta with the garlic, then brush with 1 table-spoon olive oil. Spread each surface thinly with tomato purée. Return to the grill until toasted.

4. Cover with aubergine slices and top with basil leaves, mozzarella and seasoning. Return to the grill until the cheese has melted. Drizzle over the remaining olive oil just before serving.

Italian Sage Toast

I have added fresh sage leaves to a version of that wonderful Italian invention – *Mozzarella in Carozza*, or fried mozzarella cheese sandwich. The result is a mouthwatering snack that disappears in seconds!

———— • ————

2 eggs
salt and freshly ground black pepper
4 thick slices wholemeal bread

3 tablespoons freshly chopped sage
2 × 200g (7oz) buffalo mozzarella cheeses, sliced

———— • ————

1. Beat the eggs and seasoning and pour into a shallow dish.

2. Dip the slices of bread in the egg so that they are well coated and all the egg has been absorbed.

3. Preheat the grill. Dry-fry the bread in a non-stick frying pan until golden on both sides. Remove from the pan and place on a grill tray. Sprinkle with sage.

4. Arrange the cheese on the sage-topped fried bread. Grill until bubbly. Serve at once.

Opposite: Cheese and Bean Rosti (page 63)

Mexican Tostados with Spiced Lentils and Peppers Ⓥ

I love the aroma of corn tacos or tostadas heating in the oven. I have never been to Mexico but it still seems to conjure up visions of *panchos*, *sombreros* and passionate guitar music!

———— • ————

1 large onion, peeled and finely chopped
2 cloves garlic, peeled and crushed
1 teaspoon dried thyme
1 teaspoon ground cumin
1 teaspoon ground coriander
2 tablespoons cooking oil
salt and freshly ground black pepper

225g (8oz) red or yellow split lentils
2 tablespoons tomato purée
2 teaspoons Marmite or yeast extract
600ml (1 pint) water
2 large red peppers
2 green chillies
8 tostados

———— • ————

1. Fry the onions, garlic, thyme and spices in the oil for 3–4 minutes to soften the vegetables. Add the remaining ingredients except the peppers, chillies and tostados. Stir and bring to the boil.

2. Reduce the heat and simmer for about 20–25 minutes until the lentils are softened but not mushy.

3. Meanwhile, preheat the oven and the grill. Seed the peppers then cut the flesh into squares. Cut the chillies in half and remove the seeds.

4. Grill the peppers and chillies until well seared.

5. Heat the tostados in the oven as directed on the pack.

6. Place four tostados on each of four serving plates and spread with some of the cooked lentils. Place the grilled vegetables on the top and add the rest of the lentils. Finish with another tostada.

Opposite: Egg and Courgette Bake (page 54)

Falafel in Pitta Bread Ⓥ

Chickpeas work well in this quick version of Egyptian falafel.

———— • ————

225g (8oz) canned chickpeas, drained
1 onion, peeled and minced
2 cloves garlic, peeled
1 teaspoon baking powder
1 teaspoon cumin seed
1 teaspoon coriander
2 tablespoons parsley

salt and freshly ground black pepper
1 tablespoon lemon juice
1 tablespoon plain flour
1 tablespoon fine oatmeal
vegetable oil for deep frying
4 small pitta breads
shredded lettuce and watercress

———— • ————

1. Rub the chickpeas through a sieve, or process in a food processor with the onion and garlic. Add the onion and garlic, the baking powder, spices, parsley, seasoning and lemon juice, and mix to a smooth paste. Roll into walnut sized balls.

2. Mix the flour and oatmeal together and roll the balls of chickpea mixture in it until well coated.

3. Half to three quarters fill a deep fryer with the oil and heat to 180°C/350°F. Deep-fry the falafel in batches for 5–6 minutes, until golden in colour.

4. Meanwhile, preheat the grill. Toast the pitta bread on both sides and slit open.

5. Fill the pitta bread with salad and falafel.

Pan Bagnat

In the summer these deliciously-filling rolls are sold all along the Mediterranean coast at beach cafés and stalls. They are usually filled with tuna or anchovy as well as eggs, olives, onions and tomatoes, but they lose nothing by leaving out the fishy ingredients. Traditionally, pan bagnat is wrapped firmly, and sometimes weighted, then left for an hour or so, to allow the flavours to mingle and the bread to become moist.

4 large flat rolls, baps or Italian
   ciabatta rolls
4 tablespoons extra virgin olive oil
10–12 lettuce leaves
2 large beef-steak tomatoes, thinly
   sliced

6 hard-boiled eggs, peeled and sliced
1 small onion, peeled and thinly sliced
   into rings
16–20 black olives, stoned and halved
8 large sprigs basil or Continental
   parsley

1. Cut each roll into two flat halves and brush the cut surfaces with olive oil.

2. Place the lettuce and tomatoes on the base of each roll and top with the eggs. Add onion rings, olives and basil or parsley.

3. Cover with the second half of the roll and serve.

Sweetcorn and Potato Fritters

This simple variation on the popular Jewish potato cakes, latkes, is very quick to make. It is delicious served with Yellow Tomato Salsa (page 108).

900g (2lb) potatoes, coarsely grated
175g (6oz) drained canned, or frozen,
   sweetcorn kernels

2 eggs, beaten
salt and freshly ground black pepper
1–2 tablespoons cooking oil for frying

1. Drain off any liquid from the potatoes then mix them with the sweetcorn, eggs and seasoning.

2. Heat the oil in a heavy-based frying pan and drop spoonfuls of the potato mixture into it.

3. Cook in batches, if necessary, over a low to medium heat for 4–5 minutes on each side until crisp and golden. Check that the potato in the centre is also cooked before serving with your chosen salsa.

Fennel and Potato Rosti

I became addicted to Swiss rosti on my first visit to Switzerland, and the simple potato mixture has subsequently provided an excellent base for endless variations. This one includes one of my favourite vegetables – fennel.

Buy the smallest fennel bulbs you can find as they will be far less stringy and, as there is less to discard, are much more economical than large ones.

————— • —————

3–4 small bulbs of fennel
900g (2lb) potatoes, peeled and cut
  into chunks
salt and freshly ground black pepper

1 tablespoon butter
1 onion, peeled and finely chopped
1 clove garlic, finely chopped
1 teaspoon fennel seeds

————— • —————

1. Trim the fronds from the fennel, and keep the fronds on one side. Trim the base and stems and cut in half.

2. Place the fennel halves in a pan with the potatoes and cover with water. Bring to the boil, add salt and simmer for 15 minutes until almost tender. Drain and slice both the fennel and the potato chunks.

3. Heat the butter in a heavy based non-stick frying pan and fry the onions, garlic and fennel seeds for 2–3 minutes with the fronds.

4. Layer the sliced vegetables in the pan, press down with fish-slice, sprinkling with salt and pepper. Cook over a medium heat for about 6–8 minutes until the base is brown. Turn over and cook the second side for about another 6 minutes until also well browned and the vegetables are cooked.

Cheese and Bean Rosti

This quick recipe for rosti differs from real Swiss rosti in that it is made with raw potatoes which have been grated instead of with cooked potatoes which have been boiled in their skins and left to go cold. You could use leftover potatoes. If you do you will not need the egg.

———————— • ————————

50g (2oz) butter
450g (1lb) potatoes, peeled and grated
200g (7oz) can kidney, borlotti or
   pinto beans, drained
1 egg, beaten
75g (3oz) Cheddar cheese

25g (1oz) freshly grated Parmesan
   cheese
1 tablespoon freshly chopped chives
1 tablespoon freshly chopped parsley
salt and freshly ground black pepper

———————— • ————————

1. Heat half the butter in a non-stick frying pan.

2. Mix the potatoes with all the other ingredients and spoon into the frying pan. Press well down so that it is evenly distributed over the base of the pan. Cook over a medium heat for about 10 minutes.

3. Slide the rosti on to a flat baking sheet. Melt the remaining butter in the pan and return the rosti to the pan with the cooked side up. Cook for a further 10 minutes until cooked through.

Rosti with Coddled Eggs

For this dish, another quick variation on the Swiss speciality is teamed with poached or coddled eggs. An egg coddler is a small pot with a screw top lid, which holds one or two eggs. Once filled, the coddler is immersed in a pan of boiling water to cook the eggs.

———— • ————

700g (1½ lb) potatoes, grated
1 small onion, peeled and grated
1 dessertspoon flour
5 eggs
salt and freshly ground black pepper

cooking oil

GARNISH
4 slices tomato
sprig of fresh parsley

———— • ————

1. Squeeze the grated vegetables dry and mix together well.

2. Beat the flour with one of the eggs and pour over the mixture. Season and mix again.

3. Heat a little vegetable oil in a heavy-based frying pan and spoon the potato mixture into the pan. Spread it evenly covering the whole of the base. Cook over a medium heat for 8–10 minutes.

4. Turn over with a large fish slice and cook the second side for a further 8–10 minutes.

5. Meanwhile, break the remaining eggs into buttered egg coddlers or poachers and season. Cover with a lid and coddle or poach for 5–6 minutes until cooked to your liking. Serve the eggs on top of the rosti and garnished with tomato slices and sprigs of parsley.

La Mancha-Style Vegetables with Eggs

The vegetable base of this authentic Spanish recipe has certain similarities to the better-known French *ratatouille* and *piperade*. Eggs are lightly stirred in, making it a more substantial snack. Serve with hunks of crusty bread or toasted croûtons.

———— • ————

½ onion, peeled and chopped
1 clove garlic, peeled and crushed
3 tablespoons olive oil
2 green peppers, seeded and chopped
1 red pepper, seeded and chopped

450g (1lb) tomatoes
450g (1lb) courgettes, trimmed and
    chopped
2 eggs, beaten
salt

———— • ————

1. Sauté the onion and garlic in olive oil in a frying pan until golden. Add the peppers, cover with a lid, and continue to cook gently.

2. Meanwhile, pour boiling water over the tomatoes and leave for a couple of minutes. Peel and remove seeds. Add to the pan, crushing down the vegetables with a wooden spoon. Cook, uncovered, over a low heat for about 5 minutes.

3. Add the courgettes to the other vegetables before the liquid from the tomatoes has completely evaporated. When the courgettes begin to change colour, add salt and half a teaspoon of sugar if the tomatoes seem too acid.

4. Cook over a low heat for a few more minutes until the vegetables are tender. Add the beaten eggs, stir once or twice then cook until set. Serve with crusty bread or toasted croûtons.

· CHAPTER FOUR ·

SALADS LARGE AND SMALL

HERE I have included salads which can be served as side salads with cooked dishes or as part of a medley of salads. For example, Red Cabbage and Sour Cream Salad, Apple, Date and Chicory Salad and Watercress and Pistachio Nut Salad make a very good combination.

Other recipes, such as Mustard and Brie Leafy Salad, Stuffed Pepper Salads and Orange and Goat's Cheese Salad are substantial enough for a main course.

Many of my side salads are simply made in a matter of moments using whatever I happen to have left in the salad box. To these I add an interesting dressing, such as the yoghurt-based one in Vine Salad, the dressing flavoured with balsamic vinegar that I added to the Three Fruit Salad, or the mustard-based dressing used in the Brie Leafy Salad.

Warm Carrot Salad with Rocket Ⓥ

The moors occupied the southern half of Spain for 700 years, so it's not surprising that their influence lingers on in the exotic flavours of some of the dishes, such as this carrot salad from Granada.

———— • ————

225g (8oz) carrots, sliced
4 tablespoons extra virgin olive oil
freshly ground black pepper
1 teaspoon ground cumin
75g (3oz) canned chickpeas or red
  kidney beans

juice of ½ lemon
2 tablespoons sherry vinegar
1 teaspoon clear honey
a few handfuls of rocket leaves

———— • ————

1. Place the carrots in a small pan with 1 tablespoon of the oil, the pepper and cumin. Barely cover with water and bring to the boil.

2. Cook over a medium heat for about 7 minutes until all the liquid has boiled away and the carrots are just tender. You may need to stand over it towards the end to stop the carrots burning. Remove from the heat.

3. Add the chickpeas or kidney beans to the pan and toss together. Mix the remaining oil with the lemon juice, sherry vinegar and honey and pour into the pan with the vegetables.

4. Arrange the rocket on individual serving plates and spoon on the vegetables and their dressing.

Red Cabbage and Soured Cream Salad

This makes a very colourful salad to serve when red cabbages are available. When they are not, firm green cabbage can be used instead. Grate the cabbage on a coarse grater as this gives a much better texture than trying to shred it – I never seem to be able to get it fine enough even with a sharp knife.

———— • ————

1/2 red cabbage
3 sticks celery
1 bunch spring onions

50g (2oz) walnut halves
3 tablespoons soured cream
salt and freshly ground black pepper

———— • ————

1. Coarsely grate the cabbage, and finely chop the celery and spring onions. Chop the walnuts.

2. Place all the ingredients in a large bowl and toss together.

Vine Salad ⓥ

If you live near a Greek grocer's store, or a good delicatessen, you will be able to buy vine leaves packed in brine. These make a very attractive lining for the salad bowl, but warn everyone not to eat them for they will be very tough!

———— • ————

225g (8oz) seedless white grapes, halved
7.5cm (3 inch) cucumber, diced
3 sticks of celery, finely chopped
1 small green pepper, seeded and finely chopped

1 tablespoon raisins or sultanas

DRESSING
2 tablespoons plain yoghurt
1 teaspoon lemon juice
1/4 teaspoon dried rosemary

1. Place all the salad ingredients in a bowl and toss well together.

2. Spoon into a serving dish lined, if liked, with whole vine leaves.

3. Mix the dressing ingredients together and beat with a fork. Pour over the salad and serve.

Apple, Date and Chicory Salad ⓥ

This is a very refreshing salad to serve with Sweetcorn and Potato Fritters (page 61) or Grilled Feta Cheese (page 110).

———— • ————

2 dessert apples
juice of ¼ lemon
4 large heads of chicory, sliced
50g (2oz) dates from a box, stoned and
   chopped

1 tablespoon olive oil
pinch dried mixed herbs
freshly ground black pepper

GARNISH
freshly chopped parsley

———— • ————

1. Core and quarter the apples and cut into small chunks. Toss in the lemon juice.

2. Add the remaining ingredients and toss together thoroughly.

3. Serve at once with a sprinkling of freshly chopped parsley.

Courgette Salad ⓥ

This makes a delicious starter or it can be served as a side salad or as part of a buffet. To make a more substantial dish add 4 chopped hard-boiled eggs or 125g (4oz) diced cheese such as mature Cheddar or Gouda. If you do this it will, of course, no longer be suitable for vegans.

———— • ————

450g (1lb) courgettes, trimmed and
    diced
4 tomatoes, peeled and diced
3 spring onions, trimmed and diced
1 tablespoon freshly chopped coriander

1 green chilli pepper, halved, seeded
    and chopped
2 tablespoons olive oil
1 teaspoon wine or cider vinegar
salt and freshly ground black pepper

———— • ————

1. Steam the courgettes for 3–4 minutes, drain and leave to cool.

2. Mix all ingredients together.

Italian Bean Salad ⓥ

Look for Italian borlotti beans or pinto beans for this salad from southern Italy. The beans have pretty pink strands running through the skins which look very attractive in the salad. If you cannot find them, plain cannellini beans taste almost as good.

———— • ————

1 large red pepper, cut into quarters
    and seeded
1 tablespoon capers
20 black olives, stoned and chopped
1 tablespoon freshly chopped parsley
1 × 400g (14oz) can borlotti, pinto or
    cannellini beans, drained

DRESSING
4 tablespoons extra virgin olive oil
1 tablespoon wine or cider vinegar
1 teaspoon French mustard
salt and freshly ground black pepper

———— • ————

1. Place the pepper quarters skin side up under a hot grill and cook until well charred. Remove from the heat and leave to cool a little. Peel off the charred skin and dice the flesh.

2. Mix the peppers with all the other ingredients in a large bowl.

3. Mix all the dressing ingredients together and pour over the bean salad. Serve at once.

Watercress and Pistachio Nut Salad Ⓥ

This is very much a store-cupboard salad. You can add ingredients according to what you have to hand, for example, baby artichoke hearts, onions in oil, olives, canned pimento strips, or olive paste spread on to rounds of toast.

Toasting brings out the flavours of most nuts and seeds and it is a good idea to toast more than you need for one recipe. Either place the nuts in a dry frying pan and toast over a medium heat, keeping the nuts on the move, or toast them under the grill. Take care, as most nuts burn easily.

Sun-dried tomatoes packed in oil are quicker to use than those sold dried as these must be soaked in boiling water and left to stand for 15 minutes before draining and cutting into thin strips.

———— • ————

*1 bunch of watercress or watercress
    tossed with lambs lettuce or baby
    leaves*
3 tablespoons toasted pistachio nuts
1 tablespoon toasted pine nuts
*3–4 pieces sun-dried tomatoes, cut into
    thin strips*

sprigs of fresh herbs

DRESSING
4 tablespoons extra virgin olive oil
*1 tablespoon well-flavoured vinegar
    such as sherry, tarragon or orange*
salt and freshly ground black pepper

———— • ————

1. Strew your chosen leaves over plates and sprinkle with the nuts and tomato strips. Dot with any chosen additions, and sprigs of herbs.

2. Beat dressing ingredients together and spoon on at the last minute.

Green Mango Salad

Very often mangoes arrive in the shops when they are still green. Rather than wait for them to ripen up, try this deliciously tangy salad. Serve with Curried Beans (page 100) and one of the rice dishes in Chapter 9.

———— • ————

2 tablespoons plain yoghurt
pinch salt
½ teaspoon vegetarian Worcestershire
   sauce

1 teaspoon vinegar
juice of ½ lime
1 green mango, peeled and the flesh
   grated

———— • ————

1. Mix the yoghurt, salt, Worcestershire sauce, vinegar and lime juice together.

2. Add the mango and toss well.

Orange and Date Salad ⓥ

This really clean and fresh-tasting salad comes from Morocco, where it is often served before a filling dish like couscous. It also makes an excellent side salad with Halloumi Cheese and Fennel Kebabs (page 114) or Bulgar and Nut Pilaf (page 161).

Fresh dates are used in the authentic recipe. Dried dates can be used if fresh ones are not available, but you will not need to use quite so many dates.

For an interesting variation, replace the dates with a similar quantity of stoned and chopped black olives.

———— • ————

3 large thin skinned oranges, peeled
   and pith removed
juice of 1 lemon
2 teaspoons sugar
pinch of salt

6–8 Cos lettuce leaves
50g (2oz) fresh dates (weighed after
   they are stoned), chopped
25g (1oz) blanched almonds
ground cinnamon

———— • ————

1. Cut out the orange flesh from between the segment membranes, retaining the juice.

2. Mix the retained orange juice with the lemon juice, sugar and salt.

3. Tear the lettuce leaves into pieces and carefully toss with the orange segments. Spoon into a bowl and pour over the dressing.

4. Scatter the dates and almonds over the salad then sprinkle with a little ground cinnamon. Serve at once.

Fennel and Chicory Salad Ⓥ

This salad works well as part of a salad buffet but it is also very good served with Empedrano Madrileno or Balaton Hotpot (pages 157 and 94). Alternatively, add cubes of cheese or chopped hard-boiled eggs to turn it into a main course salad (not for vegans) and serve with crusty bread or a rice salad.

———— • ————

2 small bulbs of fennel
2 heads chicory
2 apples

1 tablespoon lemon juice
2 tablespoons extra virgin olive oil
salt and freshly ground black pepper

———— • ————

1. Trim the fennel keeping any green fronds on one side. Cut the fennel bulbs into quarters.

2. Plunge the fennel quarters into boiling water and leave for 1 minute. Drain and plunge into cold water. Leave while you prepare the other ingredients.

3. Core the apples and cut into small dice. Toss in lemon juice to stop them discolouring.

4. Cut the chicory into thick strips and mix with the apples.

5. Drain the fennel and cut into thin sticks and add to the chicory and apples. Pour on the oil. Season. Toss well and serve garnished with the reserved fennel fronds.

Hungarian Salad ⓥ

All the salads I have ever had in Hungary seem to be marinated overnight in a light sweet and sour dressing which gives them a very attractive flavour. However, if you haven't time to wait you can achieve a rather similar flavour by mixing sweet and sour cucumbers, which are available in jars or loose in delicatessens, into a fresh vegetable salad. Pickling cucumbers are smaller and thinner than regular ones and have a more bitter, less sweet taste.

———— • ————

1 sweet and sour cucumber, very thinly sliced
1 small pickling cucumber, very thinly sliced
1 small red pepper, seeded

1 carrot, peeled and coarsely grated
2 tablespoons lemon juice
pinch each paprika pepper and caraway seeds

———— • ————

1. Put the sweet and sour cucumber and the fresh pickling cucumber in a bowl with a little of the liquor from the sweet and sour cucumber jar.

2. Shred the red pepper as thinly as possible and add to the bowl with the carrot. Toss with the cucumbers.

3. Add the lemon juice, paprika and caraway and leave until required.

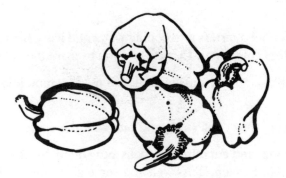

Mustard and Brie Leafy Salad

Serve this attractive salad as a main course for summer suppers or cut the quantities and serve as a first course. Follow it with Braised Spicy Aubergines and Singapore Noodles (pages 124 and 147).

————— • —————

50g (2oz) corn salad
1/2 lollo rosso lettuce
1/2 small round lettuce
7.5cm (3 inch) cucumber, finely sliced
4 × 75g (3oz) English Country Brie, sliced
12 kumquats, sliced

sprigs of fresh chervil

DRESSING
150ml (1/4 pint) olive oil
2 tablespoons lemon juice
3 tablespoons whole-grain mustard
salt and freshly ground black pepper

————— • —————

1. Arrange the corn salad, lollo rosso and round lettuce on four individual plates, keeping each one separate from the other and taking up about three-quarters of the plate. Fill in the gap with sliced cucumber.

2. Arrange the cheese just off the centre of the plate. Dot with sliced kumquats and sprigs of chervil.

3. Mix the dressing ingredients together and pour over the salad.

Orange and Goat's Cheese Salad

This salad can be made with various different kinds of goat's cheese to suit your personal preference. Choose from Roubliac fresh goat's cheese coated in herbs or paprika or a mature St Maure.

———— • ————

lettuce leaves
½ bunch watercress, trimmed
2 × 175g (6oz) small log-shaped
 goat's cheeses, sliced
2 oranges, peeled, segmented and
 trimmed
12 walnut halves, coarsely chopped

DRESSING
6 tablespoons olive oil
1 tablespoon orange juice
1 tablespoon vinegar
a little grated orange rind
salt and freshly ground black pepper

———— • ————

1. Tear the lettuce leaves into small pieces and mix with the watercress. Place on four individual plates.

2. Arrange four to five slices of goat's cheese in the centre of each plate. Place the orange segments around the cheese and sprinkle with walnuts.

3. Mix the dressing ingredients and beat well with a fork. Pour over the salad and serve at once.

Stuffed Pepper Salad

Serve these attractive pepper rings with a salad and crusty wholemeal rolls. If you do not eat both peppers, the remaining one can be stored, uncut, in the 'fridge for two to three days.

———— • ————

2 medium-sized red or green peppers
225–300g (8–10oz) full-fat soft
* cheese*
50g (2oz) mixed peanuts and raisins,
* finely chopped*
6 spring onions, trimmed finely
* chopped*
2 small sticks celery, finely chopped

1 teaspoon freshly grated root ginger
* (optional)*
salt and freshly ground black pepper

TO SERVE
mixed salad leaves
cherry tomatoes
sprigs of fresh herbs

———— • ————

1. Cut the tops off the peppers and scoop out all the seeds. Trim off any flesh from the cut tops and chop finely.

2. Place the cheese in a bowl and add the chopped pepper, the nuts and raisins, spring onions, celery, and root ginger if used. Mix well together and season to taste.

3. Spoon the cheese mixture into the scooped-out peppers and press well down.

4. Just before serving cut the stuffed peppers into slices, using a sharp knife. Arrange the mixed salad leaves on serving plates and place slices of pepper on top. Dot with cherry tomatoes and sprigs of herbs.

Courgette and Dill Moulded Salads Ⓥ

Moulded salads like this look very attractive on the plate. They make a good centrepiece for a cold meal or they can be served as a first course. Follow with Sicilian Potatoes, and Chickpeas with Spinach (pages 88 and 93). Alternatively, serve as a simple main course with jacket potatoes.

———————— • ————————

225g (8oz) courgettes, trimmed and coarsely grated
2 small carrots, peeled and finely grated
1/4 small green pepper, seeded and finely shredded

50g (2oz) low-fat soft cheese or tofu
2 tablespoons freshly chopped dill
salt and freshly ground black pepper
small mixed salad leaves

———————— • ————————

1. Mix the courgettes, carrots and green pepper together.

2. Add the cheese or tofu, the dill and seasonings and mix well.

3. Spoon the mixture into four small ramekin dishes, pressing down well as you go.

4. Turn out on a bed of small mixed salad leaves and serve at once.

Oriental Salad Platter

It is very easy to vary this dish according to the vegetables you happen to have in the kitchen. Swede or turnip can be used in place of celeriac. Another unusual mixture with a good flavour and colour is beetroot with celeriac. Shredded Chinese leaves or watercress can replace the beansprouts.

———— • ————

225g (8oz) celeriac, peeled and grated
1 carrot, peeled and grated
1 teaspoon lemon juice
1 tablespoon unrefined sesame oil or
    ordinary salad oil with a few drops
    of roasted sesame oil

4–6 spring onions, very finely chopped
1 teaspoon freshly grated root ginger
salt and freshly ground black pepper
225g (8oz) fresh soft goat's cheese
2 tablespoons toasted sesame seeds
125g (4oz) beansprouts

———— • ————

1. Mix the celeriac and carrot with the lemon juice and 1 teaspoon of the oil.

2. Add the spring onions, ginger and seasoning. Mix together and spoon into four individual ramckins, pressing down well as you go. Turn out on to four individual plates.

3. Mix the soft goat's cheese with a good grind of black pepper then shape into small balls and roll in the toasted sesame seeds.

4. Toss the beansprouts in the remaining oil and arrange round the moulded salads with the cheese balls. Serve at once.

· CHAPTER FIVE ·

TOP-OF-THE-STOVE DISHES

ALL THE recipes in this section are cooked in a single pan on the top of the stove. There is no need to heat the oven for dishes like Chilli Braised Cabbage, Braised Fennel with Rosemary or Balaton Hotpot, and Minted Tandoori Potato with Cauliflower.

I find omelettes very useful for quick meals and I have been experimenting with different fillings based on Continental and Middle Eastern cuisines. The results are quite spectacular, so do try them. I often serve these omelettes when I have friends for supper. It's quicker to make one large omelette and cut this up, than to make four or more individually cooked omelettes.

Watercress and Cottage Cheese Omelette

The cottage cheese gives a very light texture to this quickly-made omelette and the watercress gives it an interesting spicy flavour.

———— • ————

4 heaped tablespoons cottage cheese
a little crushed garlic (optional)
1/2 bunch watercress, coarsely chopped
2 tablespoons freshly grated Parmesan
cheese

6 eggs
6 tablespoons water
salt and freshly ground black pepper
sunflower or safflower oil

———— • ————

1. Mix the cottage cheese with the garlic, if using, the watercress and Parmesan cheese and keep on one side.

2. Lightly oil a large frying pan and preheat it. Beat the eggs with the water and seasoning and pour into the pan. Gently stir the egg mixture so the liquid egg flows beneath set egg, on to the base of the pan. When the omelette is lightly set, stop stirring to allow the underneath to brown slightly, but the top should remain creamy.

3. Dot with spoonfuls of the cheese and watercress mixture. Fold up and serve at once.

Iranian Omelette with Courgettes and Mint

Iranian omelettes are flat omelettes similar to Spanish *tortillas* but they are not cooked for as long and should be just a little runny in the centre. The yoghurt makes them very light and fluffy.

Other ingredients to use in place of courgettes and mint, include peas and freshly chopped chervil, diced celeriac and chopped chives or spring onions and chopped sage.

———————— • ————————

225g (8oz) courgettes, trimmed and diced
6 eggs, beaten
4 tablespoons plain yoghurt

salt and freshly ground black pepper
2 tablespoons freshly chopped mint
1 tablespoon cooking oil

———————— • ————————

1. Steam the courgettes in a steamer or a very little water for 4 minutes until just tender.

2. Beat the eggs with the yoghurt, seasoning and mint, and stir in the cooked courgettes.

3. Heat the oil in a small frying pan and pour in the egg mixture.

4. Cook over a medium heat for 2 minutes, stir once or twice then cook for a further 6–8 minutes until just set in the centre.

Leek and Walnut Omelette

The inspiration for this omelette comes from the Middle East where similar ingredients are sometimes baked in the oven to make large *tortilla*-style set omelettes. I prefer my omelettes to be a little runny in the centre so I cook them on top of the stove and remove them from the heat just before they are fully set.

———— • ————

about 20g (¾ oz) butter
450g (1lb) leeks, trimmed and finely
   chopped
75g (3oz) very coarsely chopped
   walnuts

6 eggs
1½ teaspoons turmeric
salt and freshly ground black pepper

———— • ————

1. Heat about 15g (½ oz) butter in a frying pan and add the leeks and walnuts. Gently fry over a low heat for 7 minutes until the leeks are tender.

2. Transfer to a bowl and add the other ingredients, except the remaining butter. Beat together well.

3. Add the remaining butter to the pan and heat through. Pour in the egg mixture and stir gently once or twice over a medium heat for 2–3 minutes to make the omelette. Fold over and serve.

Soufflé Omelette with Spinach and Pine Nuts

I wasn't sure whether to call this omelette 'Florentine' because the main flavouring is spinach, and in Italy dishes using spinach are often so named, or 'Roman' because the method of preparing the spinach comes from a friend in Rome. In the end I decided upon the longer but more descriptive name above!

———————— • ————————

15g (½ oz) butter
2 tablespoons pine nuts
2 tablespoons raisins
¼ teaspoon grated lemon rind

450g (1lb) young leaf spinach
6 eggs, separated
4 tablespoons water

———————— • ————————

1. Heat the butter in a saucepan and gently fry the pine nuts, raisins and lemon rind until the nuts begin to brown. Add the spinach and toss over a low heat until the spinach begins to wilt. Chop coarsely and leave to cool.

2. Beat the egg yolks with the water and spinach mixture.

3. Whisk the egg whites until they are very stiff. Stir 1 tablespoonful into the egg and spinach mixture and fold in the rest.

4. Pour into a non-stick frying pan and cook slowly over a low heat for 4–5 minutes. Preheat the grill to moderate.

5. Place the frying pan under the grill and cook for another 5 minutes until set in the centre. Serve from the pan.

Soufflé Omelette with Stir-Fried Vegetables

It really does not take very long at all to whisk up this frothy omelette. The filling can be varied according to what is in your vegetable rack!

———————— • ————————

6 eggs, separated
3 tablespoons water
salt and freshly ground black pepper

FILLING
1 tablespoon cooking oil
1/4 green pepper, seeded and cut into
    thin strips

1/4 red pepper, seeded and cut into thin
    strips
50g (2oz) mangetout, or French beans,
    stringed
50g (2oz) beansprouts
1 teaspoon soy sauce

———————— • ————————

1. Heat the oil for the filling in a wok or frying pan and stir-fry the peppers and mangetout or beans for 2 minutes. Keep on one side.

2. Beat the egg yolks with the water and seasoning. Whisk the egg whites until stiff. Stir 1 tablespoonful into the yolks and then fold in the rest.

3. Lightly oil a 25cm (10 inch) frying pan and place over a medium heat. Pour in the egg mixture and cook for about 6 minutes until just set and the base is lightly browned. Preheat the grill.

4. Finish omelette off under a hot grill.

5. Add the beansprouts and soy sauce to the stir-fry mixture and return to the heat for 1 minute. Toss together and spoon on to the omelette. Fold over and serve at once.

Glazed Garlic Tofu Ⓥ

This baste makes a very well flavoured tofu to serve with almost any of the rice dishes given in Chapter 9. I sometimes vary the flavour by adding Chinese five spice powder or toasted sesame seeds and fresh coriander. Serve with plain boiled rice or fried noodles.

———— • ————

1 head garlic, broken into cloves and
   peeled
1/4 teaspoon red pepper flakes
3 tablespoons soy sauce

150ml (1/4 pint) vinegar
3 tablespoons honey
225g (8oz) block fresh tofu

———— • ————

1. Blend the garlic, pepper flakes, soy sauce, vinegar and honey in a food processor or blender. Transfer to a saucepan and cook, stirring from time to time, for about 8 minutes until reduced by about one third.

2. Meanwhile, cut the tofu into thick strips or large cubes. Add to the garlic and vinegar mixture and poach for about 4 minutes until the tofu is heated through.

Cauliflower Provence-Style Ⓥ

The rich, herby aromas of Provence came through powerfully in the sauce for this unusual method of preparing cauliflower. It makes a real change from cauliflower cheese and it is much faster to make.

———— • ————

1 tablespoon olive oil
2 cloves garlic, peeled and finely
   chopped
1/4 teaspoon fennel seed (optional)
1 bay leaf
1 sprig rosemary or 1/4 teaspoon dried

2 tablespoons tomato purée
125ml (4 fl oz) vegetable stock
1 cauliflower, cut into large florets
25g (1oz) black olives, stoned
salt and freshly ground black pepper
2 tablespoons freshly chopped parsley

———— • ————

1. Heat the oil in a saucepan and gently fry the garlic, fennel seeds, if using, bay leaf and rosemary for about 1 minute.

2. Stir in the tomato purée and then the stock. Add the cauliflower, olives and seasoning and bring to the boil.

3. Cook over a medium heat for 10 minutes until the cauliflower is just tender, turning it in the juices from time to time.

4. Stir in the parsley and serve.

Chilli Braised Cabbage Ⓥ

Cabbage always gets a bad press but if it is treated carefully it can form the basis of quite a wide range of interesting dishes. This one comes from Hungary, where a very hot paprika pepper is used. It is quite difficult to obtain outside Hungary so I have used fresh green chilli to give the heat and a mild paprika pepper for the flavour.

———————— • ————————

1 large onion, peeled and sliced
1 green chilli, seeded and chopped
2 tablespoons olive oil
1/2 head white cabbage, shredded
4 large tomatoes, peeled and chopped

2 teaspoons paprika
juice of 1/2 lime
75ml (3 fl oz) vegetable stock
salt and freshly ground black pepper

———————— • ————————

1. Fry the onion and chilli in the oil for 4–5 minutes until lightly browned. Add the remaining ingredients and bring to the boil.

2. Cook over a medium heat, turning the vegetables from time to time, for 8 minutes until tender.

Sicilian Potatoes Ⓥ

Serve this wonderfully aromatic potato dish with a tossed green salad and finish with a plate of mature Pecorino cheese and fresh pears, and you will immediately be transported to the sunny slopes of Mount Etna.

Capers are the pickled flower heads of the caper plant and they are used a great deal as a flavouring in Southern Italy. If you find them a little strong try the milder caper fruit which are beginning to appear on delicatessen shelves.

———————— • ————————

1 onion, peeled and sliced
1 tablespoon olive oil
1 × 550g (1¼ lb) can tomatoes
16 black olives, stoned
1 heaped tablespoon capers, rinsed in
*   cold water*

1 tablespoon raisins
1 tablespoon pine nuts
2 tablespoons freshly chopped parsley
salt and freshly ground black pepper
900g (2lb) potatoes, peeled and cubed

———————— • ————————

1. Fry the onion in the oil for 4–5 minutes until lightly browned.

2. Coarsely chop the tomatoes in the can, using kitchen scissors, and add the contents of the can to the onion. Add the remaining ingredients except the potatoes. Bring to the boil.

3. Add the potatoes, reduce the heat and simmer for 25 minutes, turning the potatoes from time to time.

Californian Butter Beans ⓥ

This dish not only tastes delicious, it looks it too! Serve with stir-fried mixed vegetables and broccoli tossed with almonds for a really colourful spread. Finish this American inspired meal with a slice of Pecan Pie from your local deli.

---

1 onion, peeled and finely chopped
2 cloves garlic, peeled and crushed
2 tablespoons olive oil
1 red pepper, finely chopped
125g (4oz) button mushrooms, finely
*   chopped*

1 × 400g (14oz) can chopped
*   tomatoes*
2 tablespoons tomato purée
¼ teaspoon dried mixed herbs
salt and pepper
1 × 430g (15oz) can butter beans,
*   drained*

---

1. Gently fry the onion and garlic in the olive oil for 2–3 minutes to soften them. Add the red peppers and mushrooms and cook for a further 5 minutes, stirring frequently.

2. Add all the remaining ingredients except the beans and continue cooking over a low heat for another five minutes. Add the drained beans and cook for 10–12 minutes until the sauce thickens slightly.

Braised Fennel with Rosemary and Olives ⓥ

I came across this recipe not in Provence or Tuscany as you might expect but in New Orleans. It's surprising how strong the old European influences still are in some parts of that changing city. All the ingredients were available in the local market and the combination was the inspiration of an artist friend.

———————— • ————————

4 tablespoons extra virgin olive oil
4 whole cloves garlic, peeled
8 small bulbs (about 900g/2lb) of
*   fennel, trimmed to remove the tough*
*   and fibrous outside layers, sliced*

4 sprigs fresh rosemary or 1 teaspoon
*   dried rosemary*
12 black olives, stoned
75ml (3 fl oz) white wine

———————— • ————————

1. Heat the oil in a shallow pan and fry the cloves of garlic all over until lightly browned. Remove the cloves from the pan and keep on one side.

2. Add the fennel to the pan and brown well on both sides in the garlic flavoured oil.

3. Spread out over the base of the pan. Add the rosemary and olives and wine, and bring to the boil.

4. Cover with a lid. Reduce the heat and cook gently for 20 minutes until the fennel is cooked and most of the liquid has evaporated. Boil off any excess liquid. Serve with the reserved garlic cloves, if liked.

Opposite: Italian Bean Salad (page 70)

Beans Provençale Ⓥ

This recipe was inspired by a dish of braised celery I was served in a small restaurant just outside the amphitheatre at Orange in Provence. I think it is so good that I sometimes serve the dish as a course on its own.

———— • ————

15g (½ oz) butter
2 shallots or 4 spring onions, finely
* chopped*
1 clove of garlic, peeled and crushed
pinch each fennel seeds, dried rosemary
* and dried thyme*

3 tomatoes, peeled, seeded and chopped
450g (1lb) fresh French beans, topped
* and tailed*
salt and freshly ground black pepper

———— • ————

1. Melt the butter in a pan and gently fry the shallot or spring onions, with the garlic, fennel seeds and dried herbs for 1 minute.

2. Add the tomatoes, beans, seasoning and water. Simmer over a gentle heat for about 10–12 minutes, shaking the pan from time to time. The beans should still have a slight 'bite'.

Opposite: Cheese and Prune Purses (page 25)

Butter Bean Pots

These attractive little pots make a delicious accompaniment to Curried Tofu Strips served on a bed of Hot Tossed Cabbage (pages 115 and 125).
Alternatively serve as an unusual first course at the main meal of the day.

———— • ————

1 × 450g (1lb) can butter beans
1 small onion, peeled and finely
  chopped
25g (1oz) butter
2–3 tablespoons canned sweetcorn

1 tablespoon very finely chopped red
  pepper
150ml (¼ pint) double cream
3 tablespoons freshly chopped parsley
salt and freshly ground black pepper

———— • ————

1. Carefully tip the beans into a large sieve and wash under cold running water, taking care not to break them up. Leave to drain.

2. Heat the butter in a small pan and fry the onions until lightly browned. Add the sweetcorn, red pepper and cream and bring to the boil. Boil for 2–3 minutes and then carefully add the beans, most of the parsley and the seasoning.

3. Heat through in the boiling cream for a further 2–3 minutes. Spoon into heated ramekin dishes. Sprinkle with the remaining parsley and serve at once.

Chickpeas with Spinach ⓥ

Chickpeas, or *garbanzos* as they are known in Spain, are very popular in the tapas bars of Seville. This dish is usually served in an oval dish surrounded by triangles of bread fried in olive oil.

———— • ————

1 clove garlic, peeled and crushed
1 small onion, peeled and chopped
2 tablespoons olive oil
a few strands of saffron
3 tomatoes, skinned, seeded and
   chopped

1 × 400g (14oz) can chickpeas,
   drained
450g (1lb) spinach, washed and
   shredded

———— • ————

1. Fry the garlic and onion in the olive oil until softened. Add the saffron and fry for a further minute. Next add the tomatoes and cook for a further 2–3 minutes to make a thick paste. Add the chickpeas and mix well together.

2. Cook the spinach in a covered pan without any water for 1–2 minutes until it is almost tender.

3. Toss with the chickpeas and spoon into a bowl to serve.

Balaton Hotpot

The inspiration for this filling winter warmer is part Hungarian and part Turkish – indeed the combination is not unusual in Eastern Europe where the legacy of the Turkish occupation in the late eighteenth century has had quite an impact on culinary traditions. The rice is, of course, the Turkish contribution and the dish is often made with meat or poultry as well as beans.

———— • ————

1 onion, peeled and chopped
2 tablespoons vegetable oil
75g (3oz) long-grain rice
1 large potato (approx 250g/9oz)
1/4 teaspoon caraway seeds
1–2 teaspoons strong paprika pepper

1 tablespoon tomato purée
3 tablespoons soured cream
300ml (1/2 pint) water
salt and freshly ground black pepper
175g (6oz) canned red kidney or
  haricot beans, well drained

———— • ————

1. Gently fry the onion in the oil until lightly browned. Add the rice and fry for a further minute. Add the potato.

2. Meanwhile, mix together the remaining ingredients, except the beans.

3. Pour soured cream mixture over the rice and vegetables and bring to the boil. Reduce the heat and cover with a lid. Simmer for 20 minutes. Add the beans and cook for a further 5–8 minutes until the potatoes and rice are tender.

Creole Eggs

I like this dish served with crusty brown bread, but it can also be served with boiled rice or mashed potatoes, both of which will take about the same amount of time to cook as the eggs.

———— • ————

8 eggs
1 tablespoon vegetable oil
2 medium onions, peeled and sliced
1 green pepper, seeded and sliced
1 red pepper, seeded and sliced

2 tablespoons cornflour
450ml (³/₄ pint) milk
4 medium tomatoes, cut into quarters
salt and freshly ground black pepper
4 tablespoons freshly chopped parsley

———— • ————

1. Cook the eggs in boiling water for 10–12 minutes. Drain them and rinse in cold water.

2. Meanwhile, heat the oil in a large saucepan and gently fry the onions and peppers for 5 minutes.

3. Mix the cornflour with a little of the milk to form a smooth paste. Mix in the rest of the milk and pour over the vegetables. Bring to the boil, stirring all the time. When the mixture thickens add the tomatoes and seasonings.

4. Reduce the heat, cover and simmer for 5–6 minutes, stirring from time to time.

5. Meanwhile, peel the eggs and cut in half lengthways.

6. Add the eggs to the sauce with half the parsley. Stir gently then leave to cook for a further 3 minutes.

7. Pour into a warmed serving dish and sprinkle with the remaining parsley.

Moroccan Tagine of Swiss Chard Ⓥ

Tagine is both the North African word for stew and the name of the earthenware dish in which stews are frequently cooked. All kinds of ingredients find their way into a tagine, the inspiration coming from the state of the larder. This recipe comes from the Tehian area of Morocco, where it is often served with a simple dish of stewed lentils.

Swiss chard has spinach-type leaves with a wide stalk. Use both the leaves and the stalks for this dish.

———— • ————

1kg (2lb) Swiss chard
2 onions, peeled and chopped
4 tablespoons freshly chopped coriander
3 level tablespoons rice

6 tablespoons vegetable stock or water
4 tablespoons olive oil
1 teaspoon paprika pepper
salt and freshly ground black pepper

———— • ————

1. Wash the Swiss chard and dry well on kitchen paper. Chop finely.

2. Place all the ingredients in a heavy-based saucepan and bring to the boil.

3. Reduce the heat and simmer for 15 minutes until the vegetables and rice are tender and the mixture is thick.

Tagine of Okra and Tomatoes Ⓥ

Choose small okra for this dish which comes from the same area of Morocco as the Tagine of Swiss Chard. Take care not to overcook the okra as it can be very glutinous and stringy if it starts to break up. Serve with rice.

———— • ————

*1kg (2lb) ripe tomatoes, peeled, seeded
and chopped
2 tablespoons freshly chopped parsley
2 teaspoons paprika pepper*

*1 clove garlic, peeled and crushed
salt and freshly ground black pepper
3 tablespoons olive oil
225g (8oz) okra*

———— • ————

1. Place all the ingredients except the okra in a heavy-based saucepan over a high heat. Bring to the boil and cook for 10 minutes, stirring all the time until the tomatoes have broken down and the mixture is fairly thick.

2. Reduce the heat and add the okra, pushing it well down into the sauce. Cover with a lid and continue to simmer for 10 minutes until the okra is cooked.

Jamaican Run Down Ⓥ

I am not quite sure how this fragrant dish got its name but it seems to be a use-anything-to-hand kind of vegetable stew. The coconut and sweet potatoes complement each other well but they do need the regular potatoes to provide a balance. Otherwise you can use almost any kind of vegetables you have to hand.

———— • ————

150g (5oz) creamed coconut, cut into
small chunks
600ml (1 pint) water
1 small onion, peeled and chopped
2 carrots, peeled and diced
1 green pepper, seeded and diced
1 bay leaf
2 sprigs thyme or ¼ teaspoon dried
thyme

1 clove garlic, peeled and chopped
1 green chilli, seeded and chopped
2 medium potatoes
2 medium sweet potatoes
125g (4oz) canned kidney beans,
drained
1 teaspoon soy sauce

———— • ————

1. Place the coconut in a large pan with the water and bring to the boil, stirring frequently.

2. Add the onion, carrots, pepper, bay leaf, thyme, garlic and chilli and return to the boil. Reduce the heat and simmer, uncovered, for 10 minutes.

3. Meanwhile, peel and dice the potatoes and sweet potatoes then add to the pan, return to the boil and continue to simmer for about 18 minutes until all the vegetables are tender.

4. Add the beans and soy sauce and cook for a further 2–3 minutes to heat through. If the mixture is very runny turn up the heat and boil rapidly for this time.

Okra with Coconut Ⓥ

This is quite a dry dish from Southern India. Choose the smallest and youngest okra pods that you can find as they will be much more tender and far less stringy and gelatinous than larger, older ones. From time to time my local Middle Eastern greengrocer has tiny baby okra that are only about 1–2 cm (½–¾ inch) in length and they are delicious cooked in this way.

———— • ————

2 tablespoons corn oil
¼ teaspoon whole yellow mustard
    seeds
seeds from 3 cardamom pods
1 small onion, peeled and very finely
    chopped

½ teaspoon turmeric
225g (8oz) okra, sliced across the pods
15g (½ oz) desiccated coconut
salt

GARNISH
freshly chopped coriander leaves

———— • ————

1. Heat the oil in a pan and fry the mustard and cardamom seeds until they pop. Add the onion and fry for 1–2 minutes.

2. Add the remaining ingredients and fry for about 6–8 minutes, stirring all the time, until the okra is tender but still retains its shape. Serve garnished with chopped coriander.

Curried Beans

This straightforward curry is fairly mild so if you like your curries hot add some Tabasco sauce. Serve with potatoes sautéed with cardamom, or spiced rice, and a vegetable curry or with Minted Tandoori Potato with Cauliflower (page 102) and rice.

———— • ————

3 large cloves garlic, peeled and
   chopped
5cm (2 inch) piece fresh ginger, peeled
   and chopped
1 large onion, peeled and chopped
1 teaspoon cumin seeds
1 teaspoon coriander seeds
seeds from 4 cardamom pods
2 cloves
3 tablespoons cooking oil
1 tablespoon ground cumin

2 tablespoons ground coriander
1 × 400g (14oz) can blackeye beans,
   drained
1 × 200g (7oz) can butter beans,
   drained
225g (8oz) runner or flat green beans,
   stringed and sliced
2 tablespoons ground almonds
150g (5oz) plain yoghurt
150ml (¼ pint) stock or water

———— • ————

1. Purée the garlic, ginger and onion in a food processor or blender and keep on one side.

2. Fry the cumin, coriander and cardamom seeds and the cloves in the cooking oil for about 1 minute until they start to pop. Take care not to burn them.

3. Remove from the heat and stir in the ground spices and then the prepared purée.

4. Return to the heat and add the remaining ingredients. Stir well and bring to the boil. Reduce the heat, cover with a lid and simmer for 15 minutes.

Coconut Beans Ⓥ

This dish both looks and tastes attractive. Serve with Lentil Burgers (page 117) and rice.

---

1 clove garlic, peeled and crushed
1 tablespoon cooking oil
225g (8oz) shelled broad beans
125g (4oz) frozen French beans,
  thawed
2 tablespoons freshly chopped parsley
3 tablespoons freshly chopped basil

2 tablespoons sliced spring onion
50g (2oz) creamed coconut, chopped
200ml (7 fl oz) water
2 tablespoons dry sherry
2 teaspoons lemon juice

GARNISH
fresh basil leaves

---

1. Fry the garlic in the oil for 1 minute and then add the remaining ingredients except the lemon juice.

2. Bring to the boil and simmer for 5 minutes or until the vegetables are tender. Add the lemon juice and serve at once garnished with basil.

Minted Tandoori Potato with Cauliflower

The idea of using tandoori spice mix to flavour vegetables came to me by accident but it works very well. The addition of fresh mint and coriander adds a subtle finish to the dish, which is quite different from most curried dishes.

———— • ————

1 large onion, peeled and chopped
2 cloves garlic, peeled and chopped
3 tablespoons cooking oil
1 tablespoon tandoori spice mix
1 small cauliflower, trimmed and
*   broken into florets*

450g (1lb) potatoes, peeled and diced
3 tablespoons freshly chopped coriander
3 tablespoons freshly chopped mint
salt and freshly ground black pepper
150g (5oz) plain yoghurt
150ml (¼ pint) vegetable stock

———— • ————

1. Fry the onion and garlic in the oil for 2–3 minutes. Add the tandoori spice mix and continue frying for a further minute.

2. Add the remaining ingredients and bring to the boil. Stir and reduce the heat. Cover with a lid and simmer for 20 minutes until the vegetables are tender and most of the liquid has evaporated.

· CHAPTER SIX ·

GRILLS AND BARBECUES

THE RECIPES featured in this chapter range from simple grilled vegetables partnered by interesting sauces, to burgers, and kebabs. People often think that a vegetarian barbecue is difficult to manage, but most vegetables grill very well. You can also use tofu and cheeses which do not start to run on heating, such as halloumi and feta.

Most of the recipes in this section can be cooked under the grill in the kitchen or over a barbecue.

Grilled Courgettes with Walnut Mayonnaise

The best kind of mayonnaise is homemade but if you do not have the time or the inclination to make your own you can use a branded jar of mayonnaise for this recipe. However you will have to be careful with the amount of walnut oil that you add. I found that four tablespoons will go into four tablespoons of bought mayonnaise perfectly. Five tablespoons are just about okay, but six curdle the mayonnaise; this does not happen with homemade mayonnaise.

———— • ————

*4–6 large courgettes, trimmed and
  thickly sliced lengthways*
5–6 tablespoons walnut oil

salt and freshly ground black pepper
4 tablespoons mayonnaise

———— • ————

1. Preheat the grill. Brush the courgette slices with a tablespoon of walnut oil and season to taste.

2. Grill for about 2–3 minutes on each side until lightly charred and tender.

3. Meanwhile, beat the remaining walnut oil into the mayonnaise with a wire whisk. Serve with the grilled courgettes.

Grilled Vegetables with Pesto Mayonnaise

Many kinds of vegetables, such as sliced fennel, chicory, baby carrots and baby sweetcorn, can be used in this recipe. Start cooking the hardest vegetables first as they take the longest to cook, and add the others as you go along. Semi-cooked vegetables can be transferred from the grill rack to the base of the pan as cooking continues. In this way you should be able to prepare sufficient for four people as a starter, or two as a main course.

————— • —————

1 sweet potato, scrubbed and sliced
1 aubergine, trimmed and sliced
1 large red pepper, seeded and cut into
   8 pieces
2 courgettes, trimmed and sliced
   lengthways

2 tablespoons olive oil
4 tablespoons mayonnaise
1–2 teaspoons pesto sauce
sprigs of parsley and chervil, tarragon
   or basil

————— • —————

1. Preheat the grill. Brush the sweet potatoes and aubergine slices on both sides with oil. Place on the grill rack and grill for 2–3 minutes until lightly browned. Turn over and cook the second side for a further 2–3 minutes. Remove to the bottom of the pan.

2. Brush the pepper and courgettes with the remaining oil and place on the grill rack. Grill for about 3 minutes or until the peppers are well seared. Turn the courgette slices over once during this time.

3. Meanwhile, mix the mayonnaise and pesto sauce together and keep on one side.

4. When the vegetables are cooked, arrange on serving plates, and dot with the parsley and chervil, tarragon or basil. Serve with pesto mayonnaise on the side.

Italian Marinated Vegetables Ⓥ

Italians are very fond of vegetable antipasto dishes like this one, made by simply marinating grilled vegetables in flavoured olive oil.

———— • ————

1 red pepper, seeded and quartered
1 yellow or orange pepper, seeded and
   quartered
2–3 courgettes, trimmed and sliced
   lengthways
1 small aubergine, cut into rings
150ml (5 fl oz) extra virgin olive oil

1 clove garlic, peeled and crushed
1 tablespoon freshly chopped tarragon,
   or 1 teaspoon dried tarragon
1 tablespoon freshly chopped parsley

GARNISH
black olives

———— • ————

1. Preheat the grill. Grill the vegetables, in batches if necessary, and cook until they begin to scorch.

2. Put the peppers into a polythene bag and tie. Leave for 15 minutes and then peel off the thin but tough skins. Arrange the vegetables in a shallow dish.

3. Mix the remaining ingredients and pour over the vegetables. Leave to stand for as long as possible before serving. Serve garnished with black olives.

Grilled Aubergines with Moroccan Sauce Ⓥ

The warmth of the grilled aubergines brings out all the flavours in this piquant sauce from North Africa. Serve on its own as a first course for the best effect. Follow-up with either tagine or couscous (see pages 97 and 165).

———— • ————

*2 large aubergines, trimmed and
thickly sliced*
olive oil for brushing

MOROCCAN SAUCE
50ml (2 fl oz) olive oil
1 clove garlic, peeled and crushed

1 teaspoon freshly grated ginger
1 green chilli, seeded and chopped
1/2 teaspoon ground cumin
4 tablespoons freshly chopped coriander
1 tablespoon lemon juice
salt and freshly ground black pepper

———— • ————

1. Preheat the grill to medium hot. Brush the aubergine slices with oil and grill for 3–4 minutes until lightly browned. Turn the slices over. Grill for a further 3–4 minutes until lightly browned and cooked through.

2. Place the sauce ingredients in a food processor or blender and mix together.

3. Arrange the aubergines on four warmed places and spoon over the sauce. Serve at once.

Grilled Mushrooms with Pesto Sauce

This is one of the fastest hot dishes I know. As well as being an excellent starter it can be served with one of the rice dishes in Chapter 9.

———— • ————

8 large flat field mushrooms
1 × 50g (2oz) jar pesto sauce

freshly ground black pepper

———— • ————

1. Preheat the grill to medium hot. Wash and dry the mushrooms and spread the pesto sauce over the gills.

2. Grill for 5–6 minutes depending on the thickness of the mushrooms and how well-done you like to have them.

Grilled Mushrooms with Yellow Tomato Salsa ⓥ

I very much like the spicy flavour of this Mexican salsa. I have never come across a salsa served with mushrooms in any Mexican cookbook but the combination works very well indeed.

———— • ————

8 flat field mushrooms, washed and dried
olive oil for brushing
salt and freshly ground black pepper
1–2 cloves garlic, peeled and crushed (optional)

1 tablespoon grated lime rind
juice of 1 lime
bunch spring onions, chopped
6 tablespoons freshly chopped coriander
1 green chilli, seeded and chopped

SALSA
450g (1lb) yellow tomatoes, cherry or otherwise, finely chopped

———— • ————

1. Start by making the salsa. Mix all the salsa ingredients together in a bowl and leave to stand in the fridge while finishing the recipe.

2. Preheat the grill. Brush the mushrooms all over with oil and sprinkle with seasonings and garlic if using.

3. Grill the mushrooms for 4–5 minutes depending on the thickness of the mushrooms. Brush with more oil if required.

4. When the mushrooms are cooked through spoon a little of the salsa on to each mushroom and return to the grill for a couple of minutes.

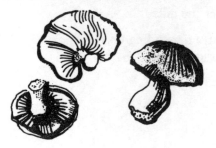

Grilled Halloumi Cheese with Balsamic Vinegar

The longer you can leave the raisins to plump up in the balsamic vinegar mixture the better the flavour will be. Serve with Potatoes with Rice (page 150) and a stir-fry dish from Chapter 7.

———————— • ————————

3 tablespoons raisins
1 tablespoon lemon juice
1 teaspoon good balsamic vinegar
225g (8oz) halloumi cheese, cut into 4
   thick slices

mixed leaves including a well
   flavoured leaf such as watercress,
   rocket or baby spinach
2 tablespoons toasted pine nuts
extra virgin olive oil

———————— • ————————

1. Preheat the grill. Place the raisins in a basin with the lemon juice and balsamic vinegar and leave to stand while preparing the rest of the recipe, or longer.

2. Grill the cheese on both sides until golden all over – about 4–5 minutes in total.

3. Arrange the mixed leaves on four plates and place the cheese on top.

4. Spoon the raisins and their juices over the cheese and add the toasted pine nuts.

5. Drizzle with olive oil and serve at once.

Grilled Feta Cheese with Olives

A dish I had in a Greek restaurant in London's Camden Town was the inspiration for this new favourite dish. The rain was streaming down the windows and the temperature was way below anything you might experience in Greece. I wanted something hot and Grilled Cheese with Olives was the answer – plus a large glass of ouzo!

———— • ————

225g (8 oz) feta cheese
6 tablespoons olive oil
2 pitta loaves, split open
grated rind and juice of ½ lemon

24 black olives, stoned and halved
freshly ground black pepper
pinch of dried thyme

———— • ————

1. Preheat the grill to medium hot. Cut the cheese into slices as far as this is possible and brush with a little of the olive oil.

2. Toast the pitta bread lightly on both sides and top with the cheese slices. Grill for a couple of minutes. Transfer to four serving plates.

3. In a saucepan, gently warm the remaining oil with the lemon rind and juice and black pepper; do not allow to become too hot.

4. Sprinkle the olives over the cheese toasts and spoon on the flavoured olive oil. Sprinkle with thyme and serve at once.

Banana Kebabs Ⓥ

Sorrel is beginning to appear in the supermarkets nowadays and its tangy sharp flavour goes very well with bananas. If I cannot find sorrel I use rocket, but the flavour is not quite so good. Serve with rice or bulgar for a main course.

———— • ————

8 baby sweetcorn
12 sorrel leaves, stalks removed
12 cherry tomatoes

3 large bananas, peeled and each cut
into 4 large chunks
salt and freshly ground black pepper

———— • ————

1. Place the baby sweetcorn in a pan of boiling water and cook for 10 minutes. Drain.

2. Meanwhile, plunge the sorrel leaves into boiling water and remove immediately. Next plunge into cold water and leave until required.

3. Wrap the sorrel leaves round the banana pieces, covering as much of the banana as possible, and thread on to skewers with the sweetcorn and cherry tomatoes.

4. Season and place under the grill or over the barbecue and cook for about 6–8 minutes, turning frequently.

Tofu Skewers Marinated in
Peanut Butter, Garlic and Lemon Ⓥ

This peanut butter marinade has a surprisingly delicate flavour. If you like a slightly stronger flavour, add a teaspoonful or two of soy sauce. Serve with rice or bulgar for a main course.

———————— • ————————

2 tablespoons peanut butter
1 clove garlic, peeled and crushed
juice of 1 lemon
2 tablespoons water

salt and freshly ground black pepper
225g (8oz) tofu
3 green peppers, seeded and cut into
*   quarters*

———————— • ————————

1. Mix the peanut butter, garlic, lemon juice and water to give a pouring consistency.

2. Cut the tofu into eight squares and marinate in the peanut butter mix for 20 minutes.

3. Preheat the grill. Meanwhile, blanch the peppers by plunging into boiling water for 3 minutes. Drain and thread on to skewers with the tofu.

4. Place the kebabs under the hot grill and cook for about 6 minutes, turning and basting with the remaining marinade from time to time.

Onion and Mushroom Kebabs Ⓥ

For an even speedier version of this recipe I use roasted baby onions packed in olive oil, instead of the raw onions, and marinated whole mushrooms. The roasted onions come from Spain or Italy, but the marinated mushrooms I prepare myself when I have some spare time. I cook them as in stage 1 below, then pack them in olive oil for later use. However you can still make the kebabs in half an hour using raw onions and mushrooms.

———— • ————

225g (8oz) small pickling onions
225g (8oz) large button mushrooms
150ml (¼ pint) white wine
1 tablespoon tomato purée
½ teaspoon fennel or celery seeds

1 bay leaf
salt and freshly ground black pepper
1 large red pepper, seeded and cut into
quarters
2 tablespoons olive oil

———— • ————

1. Preheat the grill. Place the onions, mushrooms, wine, tomato purée, fennel or celery seeds and bay leaf in a saucepan and bring to the boil. Cover with a lid and simmer for 5–8 minutes to soften the onions.

2. Grill the pepper for a minute or two but do not char. Cut into smaller pieces.

3. Thread the onions, mushrooms and peppers on to skewers and brush with oil. Season to taste.

4. Place under the grill or over a barbecue and cook for 5–6 minutes until lightly charred, turning from time to time.

Halloumi Cheese and Fennel Kebabs

Halloumi cheese grills beautifully, turning a rich golden brown. It does not drip as other cheese might and is therefore very good for barbecues. However, it only needs to be cooked lightly as it goes very tough if it is over-cooked. So make sure that the fennel is cooked to your liking before the cheese goes on the grill.

———— • ————

16 bay leaves
3 heads of fennel, trimmed and cut
   into quarters
75ml (3 fl oz) white wine

225g (8oz) halloumi cheese, cut into 8
   squares
olive oil
salt and freshly ground black pepper

———— • ————

1. Soak the bay leaves in water so that they will not burn when grilled.

2. Place the fennel in a pan with the wine. Bring to the boil and simmer for 10–12 minutes until almost tender. Drain and dry on kitchen paper.

3. Meanwhile, preheat the grill.

4. Thread the fennel on to four skewers with squares of cheese and bay leaves, placing the bay leaves on each side of every piece of cheese.

5. Grill the kebabs for 3–4 minutes, turning them from time to time so the cheese browns evenly.

Curried Tofu Strips With Coconut and Mint Chutney

If you do not have a fresh coconut, you can use 125g (4oz) desiccated coconut. Start the preparation of the dish by leaving it to soak in boiling water for 20 minutes. Then squash it dry in a sieve before using.

———————— • ————————

225g (8 oz) tofu
4 tablespoons plain yoghurt
2 cloves garlic, peeled and crushed
1 tablespoon grated fresh ginger
2–3 teaspoons mild curry powder
1 tablespoon olive oil

CHUTNEY
1 coconut

1 dried red chilli
1/2 small onion, peeled and finely
   grated
2 tablespoons cooking oil
2 teaspoons turmeric
2–3 sprigs mint, freshly chopped
juice of 2 lemons (5–6 tablespoons
   juice)

———————— • ————————

1. Cut the tofu into 4 thick strips and place on a plate. Mix together the remaining ingredients except those for the chutney, and spoon over the tofu. Leave to stand, turning the tofu from time to time until required.

2. Next make the chutney. Pierce the 'eyes' (bald patches) of the coconut with a skewer and pour out the liquid. Break the coconut open with a hammer. Ease the flesh off the shell with the point of a knife, then grate it. A medium coconut should yield about 250g (9oz) flesh. Slice the chilli lengthways and scrape out and discard the seeds. Chop the dried flesh very finely. Fry with the onion in the oil until they soften. Add the turmeric and cook for a further 2 minutes.

3. Add the coconut and mint and toss together well. Cook for a further 4 minutes, add the lemon juice and toss once more. Remove from the heat and keep on one side.

4. Meanwhile, preheat the grill. Grill the tofu strips for 4–5 minutes on each side. Serve with the chutney.

Mushroom, Carrot and Tofu Burgers with Fresh Coriander

Vegetable-based burgers taste much better if they are crisp on the outside and really moist on the inside. To achieve this I always use plenty of fresh vegetables in the mix and make sure they are grated or chopped finely so they cook evenly.

————— • —————

175g (6oz) carrots, peeled and grated
125g (4oz) mushrooms, very finely
  chopped
1 medium onion, peeled and very
  finely chopped
1 clove garlic, peeled and crushed
225g (8oz) tofu
125g (4oz) fresh wholemeal
  breadcrumbs
salt and freshly ground black pepper
25g (1oz) freshly chopped coriander
  leaves

25g (1oz) freshly chopped parsley
cooking oil for brushing
warm sesame buns

SAUCE
2 tablespoons tahina paste
2 tablespoons plain yoghurt
juice of 1 lemon
1 teaspoon sesame oil

————— • —————

1. Preheat the grill to medium. Place the vegetables in a bowl and mix together.

2. Mash the tofu with a fork and add to the vegetables with the remaining ingredients. Mix together well.

3. Shape into eight small flat burgers and brush with oil. Grill for 5 minutes on each side, brushing from time to time with a little oil.

4. Meanwhile, mix together the sauce ingredients, adding a little water if the mixture is too thick. Serve with the burgers in warm sesame buns.

Lentil Burgers Ⓥ

My father is an excellent cook and this is one of his specialities. The burgers are crispy on the outside and light and soft in the centre. He was rather vague about the quantities used to achieve this, but after a couple of testing sessions I achieved the right results.

———————— • ————————

125g (4oz) red or yellow split lentils
225g (8oz) button mushrooms,
*   chopped*
300ml (½ pint) vegetable stock

pinch mixed dried herbs
salt and freshly ground black pepper
3 tablespoons millet or oat flakes
cooking oil for brushing

———————— • ————————

1. Place all the ingredients, except the millet or oat flakes and cooking oil, in a saucepan and bring to the boil. Cover and cook over a fairly high heat for 20 minutes.

2. Mash the contents of the pan, which should be fairly dry, with a potato masher and shape into eight balls. Flatten into burgers and coat with the millet or oat flakes. Preheat the grill.

3. Brush the lentil burgers with oil and place on a piece of foil. Grill for 3–4 minutes on each side.

Grilled Aubergines with
Olive Paste and Tomatoes Ⓥ

This is one of the best recipes I know for a quick-and-easy hot after-work starter. Its rich southern Italian flavours never fail to perk up the taste buds and the spirits. I sometimes add a slice of mozzarella or goat's cheese to each slice of aubergine just before removing from the grill.

———— • ————

2 aubergines, trimmed and cut into 16
  thick slices
olive oil for brushing

1 × 125g (4oz) jar black olive paste
4 tomatoes each cut into 4 thick slices
freshly ground black pepper

———— • ————

1. Preheat the grill to medium hot. Very lightly brush the slices of aubergine with olive oil and grill for about 2–3 minutes on each side, until golden brown in colour and cooked through.

2. Spread each aubergine slice with some of the olive paste. Top with a slice of tomato and season with pepper.

3. Return to the grill and cook for another 1–2 minutes. Serve at once.

· CHAPTER SEVEN ·

STIR-FRIES AND WOK COOKERY

STIR-FRYING is a very quick method of cooking. It is important to get the wok as hot as possible before adding the food. A non-stick wok is useful for some dishes but not essential. If you do not have a wok you can use a deep-sided frying pan, preferably with rounded sides. However, you will need to take more care to keep the food on the move and to make sure that none of it sticks to the sides.

You do not need to use very much oil for stir-frying, though the temptation is to add too much. If the ingredients seem to be too dry or are starting to burn during cooking, add a tablespoon of stock, wine or water and then stir-fry over a medium to high heat.

The length of time you need to stir-fry particular vegetables depends on how crisp you like them to be. My own preference is to have root vegetables, asparagus and beans a little softer than items such as cabbage, beansprouts and mangetout.

Stir-Fried Eggs with Broccoli

Stir-fried eggs are more like scrambled eggs than an omelette, but they should not be too broken up. The method is used both in China and in Italy. In the former they are served with egg noodles and in the latter with pasta – take your pick.

———— • ————

450g (1lb) broccoli, cut into pieces
150ml (¼ pint) vegetable stock
¼ small green pepper, seeded and
    diced
¼ small red pepper, seeded and diced

2 tablespoons finely chopped spring
    onion
2 tablespoons cooking oil
4 eggs, beaten
2 tablespoons water
salt and freshly ground black pepper

———— • ————

1. Cook the broccoli in boiling vegetable stock for 3–4 minutes. Drain.

2. Meanwhile, fry the peppers and spring onions in the oil in a non-stick frying pan or wok for 2 minutes.

3. Mix the eggs, water and seasoning and pour over the top. Stir-fry for about 30 seconds. As the egg begins to set, add the broccoli, stir and serve at once.

Stir-Fried Eggs with Broad Beans and Peppers

This stir-fried egg dish is inspired by the chef of one of the Californian-style East/West restaurants which are becoming so popular. The dish is both fresh and crunchy as well as being quite creamy!

———— • ————

4 eggs, beaten
1 tablespoon milk
2 tablespoons freshly chopped parsley
salt and freshly ground black pepper
knob of butter
1 tablespoon cooking oil

2 leeks, trimmed and finely chopped
1 red pepper, seeded and chopped
350g (12oz) broad beans
1 tablespoon soy sauce
2 tablespoons vegetable stock or water
1 tablespoon sherry

———— • ————

1. Mix the eggs with the milk, parsley and seasonings.

2. Heat the butter in a non-stick wok or deep frying pan and add the eggs. Stir the eggs so they do not set into a solid mass but not so vigorously as to scramble them.

3. When the eggs are just set, transfer to a plate and keep warm.

4. Clean the pan with kitchen paper and add the oil. Stir-fry the leeks, peppers and beans for 2–3 minutes and add the remaining ingredients.

5. Continue to stir-fry over a high heat until the liquid has almost evaporated and the beans are cooked. Return the eggs to the pan, toss well and serve at once.

Tofu with Mushrooms Ⓥ

Depending on the brand of chilli bean sauce that you use, this can be quite a spicy dish – I usually choose a Szechuan black bean sauce which is pretty hot. Serve with rice for a main course.

———— • ————

450ml (¾ pint) cooking oil plus 1
    tablespoon
450g (1lb) tofu, cubed
1½ tablespoons finely chopped garlic
2 teaspoons finely chopped fresh root
    ginger
50g (2oz) spring onions, trimmed and
    cut in half lengthways

125g (4oz) button mushrooms
2 teaspoons chilli bean sauce
1½ tablespoons dry sherry
1 tablespoon soy sauce
1 teaspoon salt
½ teaspoon freshly ground black
    pepper
2 tablespoons vegetable stock or water

———— • ————

1. Heat the 450ml (¾ pint) oil in a deep-fat fryer or a large wok until it is very hot and slightly smoking. Deep-fry the tofu in batches until lightly browned. Drain on kitchen paper.

2. Heat a wok or frying pan until very hot. Add the remaining 1 tablespoon oil then the garlic, ginger and spring onions. Stir-fry for a few seconds, then add the mushrooms. Stir-fry for 30 seconds, before adding the remaining ingredients.

3. Reduce the heat to very low and add the tofu. Cover and simmer for 8 minutes.

Opposite: Californian Butter Beans (page 89) served with stir-fried mixed vegetables and broccoli tossed with slivered almonds

Stir-Fried Tofu and Garlic
in Field Mushrooms Ⓥ

This is an adaptation of another of Pete Smith's excellent recipes in *New Woman* magazine. He used shallots, but as a garlic fan, I decided to use this pungent vegetable instead. Nor did I have the time to marinate the tofu so a well-flavoured stir-fry base was very important. Here's the result.

———————— • ————————

*4 very large field mushrooms or 8
  smaller ones
2 tablespoons cooking oil
salt and freshly ground black pepper
2 tablespoons unrefined sesame oil or
  ordinary cooking oil with a few
  drops of roasted sesame oil added to
  it*

*8 whole cloves garlic, peeled
1/2 tablespoon freshly grated root ginger
1 bunch spring onions, trimmed and
  cut into 2.5cm (1 inch) lengths
1/4 teaspoon grated orange rind
2 tablespoons soy sauce
225g (8oz) fresh tofu cut into cubes*

———————— • ————————

1. Preheat the grill to medium hot. Trim the mushroom stalks. Brush the mushrooms with oil and grill for about 5 minutes on each side or until the mushrooms are beginning to soften.

2. Place the sesame oil in a non-stick wok or deep frying pan and gently fry the garlic for 5 minutes to soften it.

3. Add the ginger and spring onions and stir-fry for 30 seconds. Next add the orange rind, soy sauce and tofu cubes and toss over a high heat until well mixed. Spoon over the grilled mushrooms and serve at once with boiled rice.

Opposite: Mixed Vegetables with Cashews (page 127) and Singapore Noodles
(page 147)

Braised Spicy Aubergines ⓥ

The Chinese have always used their woks to braise food as well as to stir-fry it. The technique usually involves rather more sauce than would be used in stir-frying and a certain amount of reduction takes place. The results can be quite rich and spicy. Serve with rice or noodles.

————— • —————

2 tablespoons cooking oil
2 tablespoons finely chopped garlic
1½ tablespoons finely chopped fresh ginger
2 tablespoons finely chopped spring onions, white part only
450g (1lb) small thin aubergines, sliced
2 tablespoons dark soy sauce
1 tablespoon chilli bean sauce
1 tablespoon whole yellow bean sauce

1 tablespoon sugar
1 tablespoon cider vinegar
2 teaspoons peppercorns, roasted and ground
300ml (½ pint) vegetable stock or water

GARNISH
2 tablespoons chopped spring onions, green tops only

————— • —————

1. Heat a non-stick wok or frying pan until it is very hot. Add the oil and when it is really hot add the garlic, ginger and spring onions and stir-fry for 30 seconds. Add aubergines and stir-fry for a further minute.

2. Add the remaining ingredients and simmer, uncovered, for 10–15 minutes until tender. Increase the heat and stir until liquid has thickened. Serve sprinkled with spring onions.

Hot Tossed Cabbage ⓥ

The toasted seeds and orange juice give a wonderfully aromatic flavour to this unusual cabbage dish. Serve with rice and curries or with Jamaican Run Down or Balaton Hotpot (pages 98 and 94).

———— • ————

2 tablespoons raisins
50ml (2 fl oz) orange juice
a little grated orange rind
2 tablespoons cider vinegar
3 tablespoons sunflower or safflower oil
1 teaspoon whole cumin seeds
1 teaspoon black or yellow mustard
  seeds

1 onion, peeled and sliced
175g (6oz) green cabbage, very finely
  shredded
75g (3oz) red cabbage, very finely
  shredded

GARNISH
2 tablespoons flaked almonds, toasted

———— • ————

1. Place the raisins in a cup with the orange juice and rind and the vinegar.

2. Heat the oil in a large non-stick frying pan or wok. Fry the whole spices for about 1 minute until they begin to pop. Add the onion and cabbage and stir-fry over a medium heat for 3–4 minutes.

3. Pour on the raisins and orange juice and cook for a further 1–2 minutes. Serve hot from the pan, garnished with toasted flaked almonds.

Courgettes with Garlic and Olives Ⓥ

These flavours are closer to those of Mediterranean dishes than those of China but the combination works very well as a stir-fry and can be accompanied by simple egg noodles. Start the meal with Red Pepper Salad (page 37).

———————— • ————————

2 tablespoons olive oil
2 shallots or 4–6 spring onions,
   trimmed and finely chopped
2–3 large cloves of garlic to taste,
   peeled and sliced
450g (1lb) courgettes, trimmed and cut
   into large dice

16–20 black olives, stoned and
   chopped
salt and freshly ground black pepper
4–5 tablespoons vegetable stock
1 tablespoon dry sherry

———————— • ————————

1. Heat the oil in a non-stick wok or deep frying pan. Stir-fry the shallots or spring onions and the garlic for a minute or so over a high heat.

2. Add the courgettes and continue to stir-fry for another 2–3 minutes, depending on the size of the dice. Add the remaining ingredients and bring to the boil. Cook over a high heat for 1 minute and serve at once.

Mixed Vegetables with Cashews Ⓥ

Carrots can take quite a long time to cook in a wok and they tend to remain much harder than the other vegetables. The solution is to use a potato peeler to cut them into long, thin curls which will cook very quickly indeed.

—————— • ——————

2 tablespoons cooking oil
2.5cm (1 inch) piece fresh root ginger,
   peeled and grated
2 cloves garlic, peeled and chopped
1 onion, peeled and finely sliced
1/2 small head of celery, finely sliced
175g (6oz) French beans, stringed and
   sliced

100g (3 1/2 oz) mangetout
1 carrot, peeled and cut into strips
juice of 1 orange
1 tablespoon light soy sauce
2 tablespoons toasted cashew nuts
freshly ground black pepper

—————— • ——————

1. Heat the oil in a non-stick wok or deep frying pan and stir-fry the ginger, garlic and onion for 1 minute. Add the celery and continue to stir-fry for another 2 minutes.

2. Add the beans and stir-fry for 1 minute again. Add the mangetout and carrots and continue cooking in the same way for a further 2 minutes.

3. Add the remaining ingredients. Turn up the heat to boil the liquid and cook for 1 minute or so until the vegetables are cooked to your liking.

Eastern Leaves with
Lemon Grass and Coriander Ⓥ

The inspiration for this recipe comes from Thai cooking and it has a spicy, sweet/sour quality that is quite unusual with greens. Serve it as part of an Eastern medley of dishes with Singapore Noodles, Okra with Coconut (pages 99 and 147) and one of the spiced potato dishes.

———————— • ————————

2 tablespoons cooking oil
3 pieces of lemon grass, cut into
   5–7.5cm (2–3 inch) lengths
2 cloves of garlic, peeled and sliced
1/2 small head of Chinese leaves, sliced
bunch of Chinese greens, torn into
   large pieces

4 tablespoons white wine
1 teaspoon light soy sauce
salt and freshly ground black pepper
1/2 teaspoon sugar
1/4 teaspoon cayenne or chilli pepper
small bunch of fresh coriander, coarsely
   chopped

———————— • ————————

1. Heat the oil in a non-stick wok or deep frying pan and stir-fry the lemon grass and garlic for a minute or so.

2. Add the Chinese leaves and stir-fry for 2 minutes. Add the remaining ingredients except the coriander and bring to the boil. Cook for 1 minute and add the coriander. Cook for a further minute and serve.

Sautéed Spinach with Sun-dried Vegetables and Hazelnuts Ⓥ

I have the most wonderful delicatessen near my home which constantly seeks out and offers new ingredients for its customers to try out. As a result I have tried sun-dried aubergines and peppers as well as the more common sun-dried tomatoes. Whichever you can find will work well in this recipe, which is half Italian and half Chinese.

———— • ————

50g (2oz) sun-dried tomatoes or mixed
sun-dried vegetables
700g (1½ lb) fresh small leaf spinach,
stalks removed
2 tablespoons olive oil

1 clove garlic, peeled and crushed
salt and freshly ground black pepper
pinch nutmeg
2 tablespoons coarsely chopped
hazelnuts

———— • ————

1. Place the sun-dried vegetables in a bowl and barely cover with boiling water. Leave to stand for 10–15 minutes.

2. Thoroughly wash the spinach and dry on kitchen paper.

3. Drain the soaked vegetables, retaining the liquid, and slice thinly.

4. Heat the olive oil in a non-stick wok or deep drying pan and fry the garlic for 30 seconds. Add the spinach and sliced vegetables and stir-fry for another minute.

5. Add the remaining ingredients and a little of the soaking liquid from the vegetables. Bring to the boil and serve at once.

Braised Little Gem Lettuces Ⓥ

Little Gem lettuces remain reasonably firm when cooked in sauce and so work well in this Chinese braising recipe. You could also try radicchio or Belgian endive (chicory).

———————— • ————————

juice and grated rind of 1 orange
2 tablespoons soy sauce
1 tablespoon sherry
1 teaspoon grated fresh ginger

¼ teaspoon five spice powder
1 tablespoon raisins
4 Little Gem lettuces, cut into quarters

———————— • ————————

1. Pour the orange juice, soy sauce and sherry into a wok or frying pan and add the orange rind, ginger, five spice powder and raisins.

2. Bring to the boil and cook for 1 minute. Add the lettuce and cook over a high heat for about 2–3 minutes. The lettuces should heat through and soften a little but they should not be limp.

Asparagus and Mangetout with Lemon ⓥ

The lemony flavours of lemon grass, tamarind paste and lemons themselves are widely used in oriental cooking and I have been experimenting in matching them to different vegetables. This recipe uses fresh lemons with asparagus and mangetout to give a very clean flavour to a stir-fry dish in the Chinese style. However, you could replace the lemon with tamarind paste and add a teaspoonful of honey and some chilli pepper to give a Thai feel to the dish.

I prefer to leave the cooking liquor quite runny, but if you like you can thicken it by adding a little cornflour blended with a couple of teaspoons or so of water.

———————— • ————————

2 tablespoons cooking oil
1 lemon, very finely sliced
1 clove of garlic, crushed
350g (12oz) frozen asparagus, halved
175g (6oz) mangetout, trimmed
juice of 1 lemon

3 tablespoons vegetable stock
1 tablespoon light soy sauce
salt and freshly ground black pepper
½ teaspoon cornflour, blended with a
    couple of teaspoons water (optional)

———————— • ————————

1. Heat the oil in a wok or deep frying pan. Add the lemon slices carefully – they may spit when they hit the fat. Stir-fry for a couple of minutes.

2. Remove the lemon slices from the pan and retain about half of the thinnest, discard the rest.

3. Return the pan to the heat and add the garlic. Stir and add the vegetables. Stir-fry for 2 minutes and add the remaining ingredients, except the cornflour mixture.

4. Bring the mixture to the boil and cook over a high heat for a further 2–3 minutes. If liked, stir in the cornflour mixture and boil the liquid until thickened.

Diced Halloumi Cheese with Peas

This is a very colourful mixture to serve with fried noodles or plainly boiled bulgar. Add the cheese at the very last minute and take care not to overcook it.

———— • ————

2 tablespoons cooking oil
1 clove garlic, peeled and crushed
1 bunch spring onions, trimmed and
  coarsely chopped
1 small red pepper, seeded and finely
  diced
50g (2oz) frozen sweetcorn kernels
175g (6oz) frozen peas

1 tablespoon sherry
3 tablespoons vegetable stock
salt and freshly ground black pepper
pinch five spice powder
2 tablespoons freshly chopped parsley
1 tablespoon freshly chopped basil
175g (6oz) halloumi cheese, finely
  diced

———— • ————

1. Heat the oil in a wok or deep frying pan and stir-fry the garlic and spring onions for 1 minute.

2. Add the pepper and continue stir-frying for another 2 minutes. Next add the frozen vegetables and toss the contents of the pan together well.

3. Add the sherry and stock, seasoning and five spice powder and turn up the heat. Cook for 2–3 minutes, stirring all the time.

4. Add the remaining ingredients and toss over a high heat for about 30 seconds or so to warm through. Serve at once.

· CHAPTER EIGHT ·

PASTA AND NOODLE DISHES

PASTA is an essential item for any storecupboard as it is one of the most useful convenience foods. It does not take up much space yet expands to about three times its volume on cooking. Sauces can easily be made in the time that the pasta takes to cook.

Good Parmesan cheese adds the finishing touches to most pasta dishes, so do buy pieces cut from a whole cheese and grate it yourself at home just before you are going to use it. Avoid ready-grated Parmesan – at best it will be tired and at worst it will taste of sawdust. Parmesan cheese will keep in a cool, dry place for a long time. If your kitchen is warm, store the cheese in the 'fridge.

Chinese egg and Japanese buckwheat noodles not only give an authentic flavour to oriental dishes, but add interest to other quick meals.

Spaghettini with Peas and Herbs

This is such a simple dish to make but it is truly delicious. It comes from the Veneto area of North Eastern Italy and I first tried it in a little restaurant just off the grand canal in Venice. Butter is essential, so don't be tempted to use margarine, cooking oil or even a good olive oil.

———— • ————

450g (1lb) fresh or frozen peas
350g (12oz) dried spaghettini
75g (3oz) softened butter
4 tablespoons freshly chopped parsley
4 tablespoons freshly chopped basil

2 tablespoons freshly chopped chives
1 clove garlic, peeled and crushed
salt and freshly ground black pepper
freshly grated Parmesan cheese, to
serve

———— • ————

1. Steam fresh peas in a steamer, or in a covered saucepan with very little water, for 5–8 minutes. If you are using frozen peas, cook as directed on the pack.

2. Put the butter in a bowl and mix in the herbs and garlic.

3. Heat a large pan of water and add plenty of salt. When it boils add the spaghettini slowly taking care to keep the water on the boil. Cook for 5–6 minutes depending on the thickness of the pasta, or as directed on the pack. The pasta should be 'al dente' or just firm to the bite.

4. Drain the spaghettini well and return to the hot pan. Add the peas and herb butter and toss together. Serve at once with black pepper and Parmesan cheese.

Spaghetti with Courgettes and Mint

This recipe from Tuscany uses *nepitella* or wild mint. This is difficult to find in the UK and so I have used ordinary English cultivated mint instead. However, our mint is much stronger in flavour and whereas the original recipe calls for a whole bunch of *nepitella* I use only a few sprigs of English mint. The flavour is not quite the same but it is still very good.

———————— • ————————

*2 large cloves of garlic, peeled and
   quartered*
6 tablespoons extra virgin olive oil
4–5 sprigs of mint
350g (12oz) dried spaghetti

*4 small-to-medium courgettes,
   trimmed and sliced*
salt and freshly ground black pepper
*freshly grated Parmesan cheese, to
   serve*

———————— • ————————

1. Put the garlic and 4 tablespoons of the oil in a small bowl. Strip the leaves from the sprigs of mint and add to the bowl. Leave to stand until required.

2. Cook the spaghetti in plenty of lightly salted rapidly boiling water for 8–10 minutes, or as directed on the pack, until just tender. Drain well.

3. While the pasta is cooking fry the courgettes in the remaining oil for 8–10 minutes until they are golden all over.

4. Remove the garlic from the oil and discard. Pour the oil and mint over the pasta and add the courgettes. Toss well and serve with freshly grated Parmesan cheese and black pepper.

Spaghetti with Asparagus

This is a very delicately flavoured dish which is at its best when the English asparagus season is at its height in May and June. However, if you prefer not to use expensive fresh asparagus in this way, frozen asparagus is quite good.

———— • ————

350g (12oz) fresh or frozen asparagus
150ml (¼ pint) double cream
50ml (2 fl oz) well-flavoured vegetable
   stock
salt and freshly ground black pepper

350g (12oz) dried spaghetti
1 tablespoon olive oil
4 tablespoons freshly grated Parmesan
   cheese

———— • ————

1. Steam the asparagus in a steamer until tender – the time will vary according to the thickness of the stems. Cut off the tips and keep on one side.

2. Rub the stalks through a sieve, or purée in a blender with a little of the cream.

3. Transfer to a saucepan and add the cream and stock and bring to the boil. Cook over a fairly high heat to thicken the sauce. Season to taste.

4. Meanwhile, cook the spaghetti in plenty of lightly salted, rapidly boiling water for 8–10 minutes, or according to the directions on the pack. Drain and toss in the olive oil.

5. Pour the asparagus sauce over the pasta and toss together. Garnish with the retained asparagus spears and serve with the grated Parmesan and more black pepper.

Spaghetti with Sunflower Seeds and Sun-dried Tomatoes

This sauce always seems to be a bit too dry when you are making it, though it is fine once it is mixed with the pasta. So do avoid the temptation to add too much oil or the flavours will be diluted. Good herbs to use are sage, mint and thyme.

———————— • ————————

350g (12oz) dried spaghetti
50g (2oz) sunflower seeds
40g (1½ oz) sun-dried tomato paste
2 cloves of garlic, peeled and crushed
freshly ground black pepper

olive oil
fresh herbs, chopped or shredded
freshly grated Parmesan cheese, to
serve

———————— • ————————

1. Cook the spaghetti in plenty of lightly salted rapidly boiling water for 8–10 minutes, or according to the directions on the pack.

2. Meanwhile, toast the sunflower seeds until golden brown in a dry frying pan.

3. Allow the pan to cool slightly. Stir in the tomato paste, garlic, pepper and a little olive oil, depending on how much there is in the paste. Stir over a medium heat for about 1 minute.

4. When the spaghetti is cooked, drain it and tip into a heated serving bowl. Stir in the sauce and a handful of herbs.

5. Serve with more olive oil and freshly grated Parmesan.

Tagliatelle with Toasted Seeds and Fresh Herbs

This very simple dish from the hills above Lake Garda has a wonderful flavour and a very unusual texture. You can make it with cream or a good extra virgin olive oil, whichever you prefer.

———————— • ————————

350g (12oz) dried tagliatelle
salt
2 tablespoons pumpkin seeds
2 tablespoons sunflower seeds
2 tablespoons pine nuts

75ml (3 fl oz) double cream or extra virgin olive oil, preferably from Garda
freshly ground black pepper
freshly grated Parmesan cheese, to serve

———————— • ————————

1. Cook the pasta in plenty of rapidly boiling salted water for 6–7 minutes, or as directed on the pack.

2. Toast the seeds and pine nuts under the grill, or in a dry frying pan, until they are well browned.

3. Drain the pasta well and toss with the toasted nuts and cream or extra virgin olive oil. Serve with plenty of black pepper and Parmesan cheese.

Rigatoni with Peanut Butter Sauce

If you are a peanut butter fan you will love this sauce for chunky tubular rigatoni. Even if you do not go mad about peanut butter you should give this unusual sauce a try.

———— • ————

350g (12oz) dried rigatoni
salt
2 teaspoons olive oil
2 onions, peeled and finely chopped
2 cloves garlic, peeled and crushed
1 teaspoon grated lemon rind

4 tablespoons smooth peanut butter
250ml (8 fl oz) milk
freshly ground black pepper
4 tablespoons freshly chopped mixed
  herbs such as parsley, basil or
  tarragon

———— • ————

1. Cook the pasta in plenty of rapidly boiling salted water for 8–10 minutes or as directed on the pack.

2. Meanwhile, gently fry the onion, garlic and lemon rind in the rest of the olive oil in a large non-stick pan.

3. Gradually stir in the peanut butter and milk and bring to the boil, adding a little more milk if the sauce gets too thick.

4. Drain the rigatoni very well and add to the pan with the sauce. Toss together well and season. Serve sprinkled with the freshly chopped herbs.

Umbrian Chickpeas and Pasta Ⓥ

Chickpeas are a popular ingredient in the pasta dishes of Central Italy. Other pulses to use for a change include flageolet beans and whole lentils.

———— • ————

350g (12oz) dried pasta shapes such
  as fusilli, bows or macaroni elbows
3 tablespoons extra virgin olive oil
½ head celery, trimmed and chopped
225g (8oz) canned or cooked chickpeas
4 tablespoons dry white wine

3 tomatoes, peeled, seeded and chopped
salt and freshly ground black pepper
1 bunch chives, freshly chopped
1 tablespoon freshly chopped parsley
4 tablespoons freshly grated Parmesan
  cheese

———— • ————

1. Cook the pasta in plenty of salted, rapidly boiling water as directed on the pack.

2. Meanwhile, heat the oil in a saucepan and gently fry the celery for 4–5 minutes.

3. Add the chickpeas, wine and tomatoes and bring to the boil. Reduce the heat and simmer for a further 4–5 minutes.

4. Drain the pasta and add to the celery and chickpeas with the herbs. Toss all together and serve at once sprinkled with freshly grated Parmesan cheese and more black pepper.

Three Mushroom Pasta in Cream Sauce

Everyone loves this creamy pasta dish, which is served straight from the pan for the minimum of washing up. If you cannot find dried mushrooms or oyster or brown mushrooms use 450g (1lb) button mushrooms.

————— • —————

4 or 5 dried mushrooms
25g (1oz) pine nuts or flaked almonds
225g (8oz) plain dried noodles
50g (2oz) butter
225g (8oz) button mushrooms, sliced

125g (4oz) oyster or brown
  mushrooms, sliced
150ml (¼ pint) double cream
pinch ground nutmeg
freshly ground black pepper

————— • —————

1. Pour boiling water over the dried mushrooms and leave to stand for 10 minutes.

2. Meanwhile toast the pine nuts or almonds either under the grill, or in a hot dry frying pan, and cook the pasta in plenty of rapidly boiling salted water for 8–10 minutes or as directed on the packet. Drain well and keep warm.

3. Drain the soaking mushrooms and cut off the stalks. Slice the heads thinly. Melt the butter in a large frying pan and gently fry the three different kinds of mushroom together for about 3–4 minutes until they begin to soften.

4. Add the cream, nutmeg and seasoning and bring to the boil. Add the pasta and toss well together. Sprinkle with the toasted pine nuts or almonds and serve.

Fettuccine with Carrot and Tarragon Carbonara Sauce

The sauce should be very creamy with the eggs hardly set – too often Carbonara sauces are grainy because the eggs are overcooked. If you work quickly the eggs can be tossed with the pasta after it has been taken off the heat as there should be sufficient heat in it to cook the eggs to the right consistency.

———— • ————

2 carrots, peeled and very finely diced
1 tablespoon very finely chopped
    shallots or onions
1 tablespoon olive oil or butter
350g (12oz) dried fettuccine
3 size 1 eggs, beaten

50g (2oz) freshly grated Parmesan
    cheese
2 tablespoons freshly chopped tarragon
salt and freshly ground black pepper
freshly grated Parmesan, to serve

———— • ————

1. Cook the fettuccine in plenty of lightly salted, rapidly boiling water for about 7–8 minutes, or as directed on the pack.

2. Meanwhile, gently fry the carrots and onion in the butter or oil for about 6–7 minutes until tender.

3. Mix the eggs, cheese, tarragon and seasoning.

4. Drain the pasta and toss with the hot carrots and their fat and the egg and cheese mixture.

5. Serve at once with more Parmesan and black pepper.

Pasta with Leek and Garlic Sauce

You can use any kind of garlic-flavoured cheese for this well flavoured quickie. Boursin, Bressot or garlic roulade all work well. Serve with any kind of chunky pasta such as penne, rigatoni or fusilli for the best results.

———— • ————

350g (12oz) dried pasta
3–4 leeks trimmed and thickly sliced
1 × 175g (6oz) Boursin cheese

3 tablespoons double cream
freshly ground black pepper
2 tablespoons freshly chopped parsley

———— • ————

1. Cook your chosen pasta in plenty of lightly salted boiling water as directed on the pack.

2. Meanwhile, steam the leeks for 5–8 minutes until softened but still with a bite.

3. Heat the cheese in a small saucepan with the cream. Stir until all the cheese has melted, then bring to the boil and remove from the heat.

4. Stir in the leeks, black pepper and parsley.

5. Drain the pasta as soon as it is cooked, tip into a warm serving bowl and pour over the sauce.

Pasta Bows with Goat's Cheese Sauce

Soft goat's cheese melts easily to make an instant creamy yet slightly tangy sauce. The seeds not only add extra dimension to the flavour, but give an unusual crunchy texture. Poppy seeds are very popular in Hungary where they are used as a flavouring in sweet and savoury dishes.

———— • ————

350g (12oz) pasta bows
salt
1 onion, peeled and finely chopped
2 tablespoons cooking oil
4 tablespoons white wine
2 tablespoons vegetable or chicken stock
175g (6oz) fresh goat's cheese such as Perroche or Pyramid, cut into small chunks

freshly ground black pepper
1 tablespoon poppy seeds or sesame seeds
freshly grated hard goat's cheese or Pecorino cheese, to serve

———— • ————

1. Cook the pasta in plenty of lightly salted, rapidly boiling water for 7–8 minutes or as directed on the pack.

2. Toast the poppy seeds or the sesame seeds in a dry frying pan over a medium heat for about a minute or so. Keep on one side.

3. Gently fry the onion in the oil for 2–3 minutes until softened but do not allow to brown.

4. Add the wine and stock to the onion and stir in the cheese. When the cheese has melted completely, stir in the black pepper and poppy seeds and heat through.

5. Drain the cooked pasta and toss with the sauce. Serve with freshly ground black pepper and grated hard goat's cheese or Pecorino cheese.

Fusilli with Wild Mushrooms and Cannellini Beans

This pasta dish comes from Verona and is usually only served when fresh *porcini* (cep) mushrooms are in season. However, I make it all the year round with dried mushrooms of one kind or another. The flavour does of course vary depending on the type used but it is always very good.

—————— • ——————

15g (½ oz) dried porcini or ceps, or
  other dried mushrooms
350g (12oz) dried fusilli
1 small onion, peeled and coarsely
  chopped
2 cloves garlic, peeled and crushed
2 tablespoons olive oil
1 small carrot, peeled and finely
  chopped

1 stick celery, finely chopped
1 × 225g (8oz) drained canned or
  cooked cannellini beans
1 teaspoon tomato purée
2 tablespoons white wine
salt and freshly ground black pepper
1 sprig sage
freshly grated Parmesan cheese to serve

—————— • ——————

1. Put the mushrooms to soak for about 20 minutes, in just enough boiling water to cover them.

2. Cook the pasta in plenty of lightly salted, rapidly boiling water for 7–8 minutes, or as directed on the pack.

3. Meanwhile, fry the onion and garlic in the oil for 3–4 minutes until lightly browned. Add the carrots and cook for a further 3–4 minutes.

4. Add the cannellini beans, tomato purée, mushrooms with their soaking water and the wine. Bring to the boil and simmer for 10 minutes until the vegetables are cooked. Season to taste.

5. Drain the cooked pasta and toss with the sage and cooked vegetables. Serve with freshly grated Parmesan cheese.

Ravioli and Aubergine Saucers

Here's a great way to pep up canned ravioli. It makes a really good lunch or supper dish. Individual saucers can be frozen before cooking, then thawed and used later.

———— • ————

1 large aubergine, sliced
2 tablespoons cooking oil
1 × 400g (14oz) can ravioli in
  tomato sauce

300ml (½ pint) soured cream or
  Greek yoghurt
75g (3oz) fresh breadcrumbs
75g (3oz) Cheddar cheese, grated

———— • ————

1. Preheat the grill. Grease four ovenproof saucers or small entrée or gratin dishes.

2. Brush the aubergine slices on each side with oil and grill for 2–3 minutes a side or until lightly browned and tender.

3. Meanwhile, heat the ravioli in a saucepan.

4. Arrange the aubergine slices on the four prepared saucers or dishes. Spoon on the ravioli and then the soured cream or yoghurt. Mix the breadcrumbs and cheese and sprinkle over the top. Grill for 5–6 minutes.

Fried Egg Noodles

This is my slightly simplified version of an authentic Indonesian noodle dish. It can be served with almost any of the recipes in the Stir-fries and Wok Cookery chapter.

———— • ————

2 tablespoons cooking oil
2 eggs, beaten
225g (8oz) Chinese egg noodles
1 clove garlic, peeled and crushed
2 lumps stem ginger, finely chopped
1 onion, peeled and finely chopped

2 sticks celery, finely sliced
1 tablespoon soy sauce
2 tablespoons sherry
1 bunch spring onions, trimmed and
  sliced lengthways

1. Heat 1 tablespoon of oil in a frying pan and pour in the beaten eggs. Allow the eggs to spread out to make a large flat omelette. When it is cooked through remove from the pan and cut into strips. Keep warm.

2. Cook the noodles in lightly salted rapidly boiling water for 5 minutes or as directed on the pack. Drain and keep on one side.

3. Meanwhile, fry the garlic, ginger, onion and celery in the cooking oil for about 5–8 minutes, stirring all the time, until tender.

4. Add the soy sauce, sherry and noodles. Heat through, stirring well to distribute the sauce among the noodles.

5. Serve garnished with slices of spring onion and the omelette strips.

Singapore Noodles ⓥ

Every Chinese restaurant I have ever been to seems to have its own recipe for Singapore Noodles but the flavouring they all have in common is red chillies.

The basic recipe makes an excellent partner to most stir-fry dishes, or for dishes such as Chickpeas with Spinach or Tagine of Okra and Tomatoes (pages 93 and 97). Alternatively you can add any or all of the optional extras to make an even more interesting dish to serve on its own.

———— • ————

225g (8oz) Chinese egg noodles
225g (8oz) beansprouts
1 tablespoon cooking oil
1 teaspoon soy sauce
2–3 fresh red chillies, seeded and very
finely sliced

OPTIONAL EXTRAS
½ teaspoon sesame oil
2 tablespoons cooked peas
2 tablespoons cooked sweetcorn kernels
2 tablespoons diced bamboo shoots
50g (2oz) blanched mangetout
1 bunch spring onions, trimmed and
sliced in half lengthways

———— • ————

1. Cook the noodles in plenty of rapidly boiling water as directed on the pack. Drain well.

2. Heat the oil in a large pan and toss in the beansprouts. Add the noodles, soy sauce and optional extras, if using, and toss together. Heat through, add the chillies and serve at once.

Japanese Buckwheat Noodles with Tamari Sauce, Ginger and Spring Onions Ⓥ

Japanese buckwheat noodles can be used in much the same way as Chinese egg noodles. They have a good flavour of their own and need punchy flavours to go with them. Tamari is Japanese soy sauce.

———— • ————

300g (10oz) Japanese buckwheat
  noodles
2 tablespoons freshly grated root ginger
2 cloves garlic, peeled and crushed

2–3 spring onions, finely chopped
2 tablespoons cooking oil
3 tablespoons tamari sauce
freshly ground black pepper

———— • ————

1. Cook the noodles as directed on the pack.

2. Heat the cooking oil in a wok or deep frying pan and add the ginger, garlic and spring onions. Stir-fry for 2 minutes.

3. Add the drained noodles and stir-fry for another minute or so. Add the tamari sauce and black pepper and bring to the boil. Serve at once.

· CHAPTER NINE ·

RICE AND CEREAL DISHES

RICE AND cereals, such as bulgar and couscous, join pasta and noodles as convenience foods *par excellence*. They are all very easy to cook and only require double their volume of boiling liquid.

Cooking times for the rice recipes are based on white rice. If you prefer to use brown rice you may need to add a little more water and to increase the cooking times by 5–10 minutes depending upon the type of brown rice you have bought. Check the instructions on the pack.

The risottos are best made with Italian Arborio or risotto rice. These give a creamier, more authentic result than American or Basmati rice which remain a little too separate.

The recipes in this section are taken from all around the world. There is Empedrado Madrileno from Spain, Polenta Rustica from Italy, Couscous from Morocco and Spicy Corn Pilaf from the US. Most of them can be eaten on their own with a simple side salad or with grilled vegetables.

Potatoes with Rice ⓥ

This is a very useful dish to serve with all kinds of oriental food. You can pep it up a bit by adding more freshly chopped herbs, such as mint or sage, or a teaspoon of hot paprika with the courgettes and potatoes.

———— • ————

1 tablespoon cooking oil
½ onion, peeled and chopped
175g (6oz) long-grain rice
1 tablespoon freshly chopped parsley

600ml (1 pint) vegetable stock
700g (1½ lb) potatoes, peeled and
   diced
1 large courgette, diced

———— • ————

1. Heat the oil in a pan and add the onion. Fry for 4–5 minutes until the onion starts to brown. Add the rice and fry for a further minute or so.

2. Add the parsley and the stock, bring to the boil and cook for 12–15 minutes until all the liquid has been absorbed and the rice is tender.

3. Meanwhile, steam the potatoes and courgette separately in a steamer, or a very little lightly salted water in a covered saucepan, for about 10–15 minutes until cooked.

4. Stir the potatoes and courgettes into the rice and serve.

Turkish Rice Ⓥ

This wonderfully aromatic rice dish is good enough to eat on its own. It is also very good served with the Halloumi Cheese and Fennel Kebabs (page 114).

Pistachio nuts are well worth searching out as they give an authentic flavour to the dish.

———— • ————

2–3 tablespoons olive oil
1 small onion, peeled and very finely
   chopped
225g (8oz) long-grain rice
1 teaspoon salt
freshly ground black pepper
1 tomato, peeled, seeded and finely
   chopped
2 tablespoons pine nuts

1 tablespoon pistachio nuts, roughly
   chopped (optional)
25g (1oz) raisins
1 tablespoon freshly chopped parsley
1/2 tablespoon freshly chopped sage
1/2 tablespoon freshly chopped mint
1/4 teaspoon ground mixed spice
450ml (15 fl oz) vegetable stock

———— • ————

1. Heat most of the oil in a large pan. Add the onion and rice and fry gently for 2 minutes, stirring all the time. Add the remaining ingredients except the stock, and continue frying and stirring for another 3 minutes.

2. Pour on the stock, bring to the boil and cover with a lid. Cook over the lowest possible heat for 12–15 minutes, until the rice is tender and all the liquid is absorbed. Remove the pan from the heat.

3. Leave to stand for 5 minutes. Add the remaining oil and serve.

Mexican Rice

This spicy rice dish is so good I often eat it on its own with a green salad. It also makes a good accompaniment to simple kebabs or grilled burgers.

———————— • ————————

15g (½ oz) butter
225g (8oz) long-grain rice
1 × 400g (14oz) can tomatoes
300ml (½ pint) vegetable stock
salt and freshly ground black pepper

½–1 teaspoon ground chilli powder
1 red and 1 green pepper, sliced into
*   rings and seeds removed*
1 onion, peeled and sliced

———————— • ————————

1. Melt the butter in a non-stick pan. Fry the rice and add the contents of the can of tomatoes, the stock, and seasoning and chilli powder to taste. Bring to the boil and stir.

2. Lay the peppers and onions on top. Cover the pan with a lid and simmer for 15 minutes until all the liquid has been absorbed and the rice is tender.

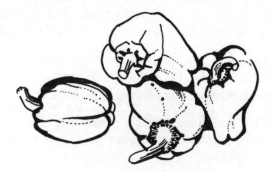

Egyptian Rice

Rice is surprisingly popular in Egypt but the spicing is quite different from that used in other parts of the Eastern Mediterranean. This is another rice recipe that is substantial enough to eat as a main course, accompanied, perhaps, by a simple tossed green salad. However, there is no reason why you should not serve it with one of the simpler stir-fries in Chapter 7.

---

1 onion, peeled and finely chopped
25g (1oz) butter
1 clove garlic, peeled and chopped
1 tablespoon freshly chopped coriander
1 tablespoon freshly chopped basil
  (optional)
1/4 teaspoon turmeric
1/4 teaspoon dried thyme

1/4 teaspoon cayenne pepper
salt and freshly ground black pepper
50g (2oz) chopped raisins
50g (2oz) chopped almonds
225g (8oz) long-grain rice
450ml (15 fl oz) water
50g (2oz) vermicelli or spaghetti
1 tablespoon olive oil

---

1. Fry the onion in the butter in a heavy-based pan until it turns golden brown.

2. Add the remaining ingredients except the vermicelli or spaghetti and olive oil. Bring to the boil. Stir and cover with a lid.

3. Reduce the heat and simmer for 15 minutes until all the liquid has been absorbed and the rice is tender.

4. Meanwhile, break the vermicelli or spaghetti into short lengths and cook in plenty of rapidly boiling salted water for about 6–8 minutes until tender.

5. Drain very well and dry thoroughly. Heat the oil in a small pan and fry the cooked pasta until golden.

6. Fluff up the rice with a fork and stir in the fried pasta.

Egg and Cardamom Pilaf with Carrots

This is the kind of pilaf which can be served on its own or with one other dish. One of my favourite choices is Okra with Coconut (page 99) – there is something very seductive about the combination of cardamom, raisin and coconut. A green salad makes a good accompaniment.

————— • —————

4 onions, peeled
4 tablespoons cooking oil
225g (8oz) long-grain rice
2 carrots, peeled and coarsely grated
2 tablespoons raisins
450ml (¾ pint) vegetable stock

1 tablespoon finely chopped parsley
1 tablespoon finely chopped mint
3–4 cardamom pods
salt and freshly ground black pepper
6 eggs

————— • —————

1. Very finely chop two of the onions and keep the rest on one side.

2. Fry the chopped onions in half the oil until they turn transparent. Add the rice and fry for a further 1–2 minutes, stirring all the time.

3. Add the carrot, raisins, stock, herbs and seasoning. Bring to the boil, cover and simmer until all the liquid has been absorbed. Remove from the heat and stir. Replace the lid and stand in a warm place for 15 minutes.

4. Meanwhile, cook the eggs in boiling water for 10–12 minutes. Drain, rinse in cold water, then peel and slice them. Slice the remaining onions into rings.

5. Remove the seeds from the cardamom pods and fry in the rest of the oil over a high heat for 30 seconds. Add the sliced onion and continue frying until they are brown but still crisp.

6. Fork up the rice and pile on to heated plates. Top with sliced hard-boiled eggs and onion rings.

Spanish Rice with Peppers Ⓥ

This extremely simple rice dish is typical of the resourcefulness of regional cooking in the poorer areas of Spain, and it works beautifully. In the Extramadura region it is traditionally prepared in large quantities with whole peppers, but for more speedy cooking, the peppers can be cut into strips before frying, as I have done here.

½ small onion, peeled and chopped
3 tablespoons olive oil
225g (8oz) long-grain rice
2 small green peppers, seeded and cut into strips

1 red pepper, seeded and cut into strips
salt and white pepper
a few strands of saffron
475ml (16 fl oz) water

1. Fry the onion in the oil until golden.

2. Stir in the rice, turning well with a wooden spoon. Add the peppers, seasoning and saffron.

3. Pour on the water and bring to the boil. Stir, cover then lower the heat and simmer for 15 minutes until the rice is tender and all the liquid has been absorbed.

Rice with Pumpkin and Raisins ⓥ

This easy Spanish recipe is from the island of Ibiza. It is quite sweet and goes well with Banana Kebabs (page 111). The best kind of rice to use is Italian risotto rice as it is more like Spanish rice than American, Patna or Basmati varieties. The end result should be drier than a risotto but softer and stickier than a pilau or pilaf.

———————— • ————————

1 tablespoon olive oil
1 clove garlic, peeled and finely
  chopped
175g (6oz) piece of pumpkin, weighed
  without the skin and seeds, diced
1 tablespoon raisins

salt and freshly ground black pepper
600ml (1 pint) vegetable stock
300g (10oz) risotto rice
pinch each of ground cinnamon and
  sugar

———————— • ————————

1. Heat the oil in a pan and fry the garlic for a minute or so until golden.

2. Add the pumpkin, the raisins and seasoning. Stir and add the stock.

3. Bring to the boil and simmer for 2–3 minutes. Add the rice, cinnamon and sugar and return to the boil. Stir and cover with a lid. Reduce the heat and simmer for 12–15 minutes until the rice is tender and all the liquid has been absorbed.

4. Leave to stand for 3–4 minutes before serving.

Empedrado Madrileno Ⓥ

This dish gets its name from the old method of dry-stone building used for Spanish houses. Small pebbles or gravel were pushed into the cracks between the stones and it is said that the beans, with their red colour, resemble the stones while the rice looks like the gravel in between.

―――――――― • ――――――――

1 × 400g (14oz) can borlotti or red
   kidney beans, drained
75g (3oz) basmati rice
2 onions, peeled and chopped
1 clove garlic, peeled and chopped

1 bay leaf
pinch salt
175ml (6 fl oz) water
2 tablespoons olive oil
1 tablespoon paprika pepper

―――――――― • ――――――――

1. Place the beans and rice in a saucepan and stir in half the onion, the garlic, bay leaf and seasoning.

2. Pour on the water and bring to the boil. Stir once and cover with a lid. Reduce the heat and simmer for 12–15 minutes until the rice is tender and all the water has been absorbed.

3. Meanwhile, fry the remaining onion with the paprika pepper, in the oil for 4 minutes, until lightly browned.

4. Stir the fried onion into the beans and rice and cook for another 5 minutes.

Spicy Corn Pilaf Ⓥ

A friend of mine in the American Mid-West is addicted to Tabasco sauce and sweetcorn, and this is one of her concoctions using them. The result is a piquant rice which goes well with kebabs.

———— • ————

1 onion, peeled and chopped
2 tablespoons cooking oil
225g (8oz) basmati rice
75g (3oz) sweetcorn kernels
½ small red pepper, seeded and finely
  chopped
½ teaspoon ground cinnamon

1 tablespoon freshly chopped mixed
  herbs
5–6 drops of Tabasco sauce or
  ½–1 teaspoon chilli powder
salt and freshly ground black pepper
350ml (12 fl oz) vegetable stock or
  water

———— • ————

1. Fry the onion in the oil until lightly browned. Add the rice and stir well.

2. Add the remaining ingredients and bring to the boil. Stir and reduce the heat.

3. Cover and simmer for 12–15 minutes until all the liquid has been absorbed and the rice is tender.

Venetian Risotto

Green peas and fennel are both popular vegetables in the Veneto region of North East Italy and here they work together to make an excellent risotto.

———— • ————

2 tablespoons olive oil
25g (1oz) butter
2 small red onions, peeled and minced
1 clove garlic, peeled and crushed
1 small bulb of fennel, trimmed and
    finely chopped
2 tablespoons freshly chopped parsley

225g (8oz) risotto rice
75g (3oz) frozen peas
125ml (4 fl oz) dry white wine
salt and freshly ground black pepper
550ml (18 fl oz) vegetable stock
butter and freshly grated Parmesan
    cheese, to serve

———— • ————

1. Heat the olive oil and butter in a saucepan and gently cook the onions, garlic and fennel for 3–4 minutes until they begin to brown.

2. Add the parsley, rice, peas, wine and seasoning. Bring to the boil then reduce the heat and cook, uncovered, for about 10 minutes until most of the liquid has been absorbed, stirring from time to time.

3. Add half the stock and return to the boil. Continue cooking and stirring from time to time. When most of the liquid has been absorbed, repeat with the remaining stock.

4. Cook until the remaining liquid is absorbed, stirring occasionally. The risotto should be slightly creamy but not wet. Total cooking time from adding the rice will be about 25–30 minutes. Serve with a knob of butter and a sprinkling of freshly grated Parmesan cheese.

Asparagus Risotto

Frozen asparagus is a much better choice for this recipe than canned asparagus, which is just too soft to withstand cooking in a risotto. Freshly steamed asparagus can be used in season if you are happy to pay the price.

———— • ————

1 × 285g (8oz) packet frozen
  asparagus, thawed
2 shallots or 4–5 spring onions,
  chopped
15g (½ oz) butter

2 tablespoons olive oil
225g (8oz) risotto rice
75ml (3 fl oz) dry white wine
600ml (1 pint) vegetable stock
salt and freshly ground black pepper

———— • ————

1. Cut the tips from the asparagus and carefully steam them until just tender. Keep to one side.

2. Meanwhile, chop the uncooked stems then gently fry with the shallots or spring onions in the butter and oil for 2–3 minutes. Do not allow the vegetables to brown.

3. Add the rice and wine and bring to the boil. Reduce the heat and cook, uncovered, until most of the liquid has been absorbed, stirring occasionally.

4. Add half the stock and return to the boil. Continue to cook over a low to medium heat, stirring from time to time.

5. When the liquid has been absorbed repeat with the remaining stock.

6. Cook until the remaining liquid is absorbed, stirring occasionally. The risotto should be slightly creamy but not wet. Stir in the asparagus tips and seasoning and serve.

Caribbean Banana Risotto Ⓥ

This has a more African than European feel to it and is very good served sprinkled with toasted pine nuts.

———— • ————

1 bunch spring onions
2.5cm (1 inch) piece of fresh root
  ginger, peeled and grated
2 tablespoons cooking oil
a few drops roasted sesame oil
¼ teaspoon ground allspice

1 fresh green chilli, seeded and finely
  sliced
225g (8oz) risotto rice
550ml (18 fl oz) vegetable stock
salt and freshly ground black pepper
1 large banana

———— • ————

1. Gently fry the spring onions and ginger in the cooking oil and sesame oil for 2–3 minutes.

2. Add the allspice, chilli and rice. Stir well and add half the stock. Bring to the boil and cook, uncovered, for about 10 minutes, stirring from time to time. Do not allow the mixture to dry out.

3. Add the rest of the stock and the seasoning and return to the boil. Continue to cook for about 10 minutes.

4. Peel and dice the banana, stir into the rice and continue cooking for a further 5 minutes until the rice is tender, the liquid has been absorbed and the risotto is quite creamy.

Bulgar and Nut Pilaf Ⓥ

Make sure that you buy easy-cook bulgar and not cracked wheat, which is slow to cook. Serve with a tossed salad.

———— • ————

1 small onion, peeled and chopped
2 tablespoons cooking oil
1 small green pepper, seeded and
  chopped
125g (4oz) canned or cooked red
  kidney beans

50g (2oz) cashew nuts, toasted under
  the grill
175g (6oz) bulgar
salt and freshly ground black pepper
350ml (12 fl oz) vegetable stock

———— • ————

1. Fry the onion in the oil for 2–3 minutes. Add the pepper and cook for a further minute or two.

2. Add the remaining ingredients and bring to the boil, stir and cover.

3. Reduce the heat and simmer for 12–15 minutes until the bulgar is cooked through and all the liquid has been absorbed.

4. Fluff up with a fork and serve.

Bulgar with Fresh Herbs Ⓥ

This is really a hot version of tabbouleh, though the ratio of bulgar to parsley is higher. It is delicious eaten on its own or it can be served with kebabs.

———— • ————

1 bunch spring onions, trimmed and
  chopped
2 tablespoons cooking oil
2 tomatoes, peeled, seeded and chopped
225g (8oz) bulgar

salt and freshly ground black pepper
475ml (16 fl oz) vegetable stock
6 tablespoons freshly chopped parsley
1 tablespoon freshly chopped mint

———— • ————

1. Gently fry the spring onions in the oil for 2–3 minutes.

2. Stir in the tomato, bulgar, seasoning and stock.

3. Bring to the boil, stir and cover. Reduce the heat and cook for 12–15 minutes until the bulgar is cooked and all the liquid has been absorbed. Stir in the herbs.

4. Fluff up with a fork and serve.

Couscous with Hot Spiced Vegetable Ragout

Couscous is the staple food of North Africa. It looks a little like bulgar but is actually tiny balls of semolina. It needs to be soaked for 15 minutes before cooking, but it cooks very quickly, and while it is soaking the accompanying Ragout is being made. Harissa is a fiery, chilli-based sauce from Tunisia.

———— • ————

COUSCOUS
225g (8oz) couscous
250ml (8 fl oz) water
15g (½ oz) butter
pinch ground cinnamon

RAGOUT
600ml (1 pint) water
4 carrots, peeled and sliced
125g (4oz) canned or cooked chickpeas
8 small onions

450g (1lb) runner beans, cut into 1cm
(½ inch) pieces
1 green or red pepper, seeded and cut
into 1cm (½ inch) pieces
4 courgettes, trimmed and cut into 1cm
(½ inch) slices
a few coriander leaves
1 tablespoon passata
1 teaspoon paprika
about 1 teaspoon harissa or chilli sauce
or ½ teaspoon cayenne pepper
salt

———— • ————

1. Put the couscous into a bowl, pour on the water and mix thoroughly. Leave for 15 minutes, stirring occasionally. Drain well in a sieve or colander.

2. Melt the butter for the couscous in a frying pan and add the couscous and cinnamon; initially it may stick a little. Keep stirring until it is hot and the grains are dry and separate.

3. Put the couscous mixture in the top of a steamer and place over gently boiling water. Cover with a lid and steam for 20–25 minutes when the couscous should be light and fluffy.

4. Meanwhile start to cook the ragout. Bring the water to the boil, then add the carrots, chickpeas and onions. Cook for 10 minutes. Add the runner beans, pepper and courgettes. Cover and cook for about 5 minutes until the vegetables are just tender.

5. Stir in the coriander, passata, paprika and harissa, chilli sauce or cayenne pepper. Salt to taste. Lightly fluff up the couscous with a fork and serve with the ragout.

Broad Bean and Okra Couscous Ⓥ

Broad beans are found in most traditional couscous dishes of Morocco. Here they are mixed with okra and tomatoes to give a fragrant topping for the couscous. I sometimes use canned lima beans in place of frozen broad beans, which makes the dish even faster to prepare.

———— • ————

225g (8oz) couscous
250ml (8 fl oz) warm water
15g (½ oz) butter

TOPPING
1 onion, peeled and chopped
2 tablespoons cooking oil
1 × 225g (8oz) can chopped tomatoes

350g (12oz) small okra, trimmed
pinch each cinnamon, ground
* coriander and dried thyme*
1 bay leaf
salt and freshly ground black pepper
175g (6oz) frozen or fresh broad beans

———— • ————

1. Put the couscous in a bowl, pour on the warm water and mix thoroughly. Leave for 10 minutes. Transfer to the top of a steamer and place over gently boiling water. Cover with a lid and leave to steam for about 20–25 minutes when the couscous should be light and fluffy.

2. Meanwhile, make the topping. Fry the onion in the oil for 2–3 minutes. Add the contents of the can of tomatoes and bring to the boil. Reduce the heat and add the okra, spices, bay leaf and seasoning. Simmer for 10 minutes.

3. Melt the butter in a frying pan, add the couscous and stir until hot and the grains are dry and separate. It may stick a little at first.

4. Add the beans to the topping and return to the boil. Simmer for a further 8–10 minutes.

5. Fluff the couscous up with a fork and serve with the beans and okra spooned over the top.

Tagine of Tomato and Egg

In North Africa eggs are rarely used in restaurant dishes, but they are sometimes used in the home, and hard-boiled eggs with cumin are sold as street snacks. This recipe comes from a family originally based in Algeria. It is usually served with couscous but you could accompany with bulgar or savoury rice instead.

———— • ————

6 eggs
1 clove garlic
1 tablespoon olive oil
450g (1lb) tomatoes, peeled, seeded
    and chopped

3 shallots or ½ small onion, peeled
    and finely chopped
salt and freshly ground black pepper
¼ teaspoon ground cumin
cooked couscous, bulgar or savoury rice,
    to accompany

———— • ————

1. Cook two of the eggs in boiling water for 10–12 minutes. Drain, cover with cold water until cool enough to handle, then peel and roughly chop.

2. Meanwhile, rub a small heavy-based pan with the clove of garlic.

3. Add the oil, tomatoes and onion and cook over a medium heat for 15 minutes, stirring from time to time, until thick and mushy.

4. Beat the remaining eggs and add to the tomato mixture with the seasonings and cumin. Stir and allow to gently scramble for 2–3 minutes until not quite set.

5. Add the chopped eggs and cook for a further minute. The mixture should not be too set. Serve at once or the mixture will go hard.

Polenta Rustica

It is well worth looking for fast-cooking polenta or cornmeal because it really is ready in minutes and there is no need to stand over it stirring as you have to when using ordinary cornmeal. I first enjoyed polenta in the Val d'Aorta in North Western Italy, where it is the staple food and there it is flavoured with the local Fontina cheese. In other parts of Italy Taleggio cheese is used. If you cannot find these cheeses, substitute Brie. Serve with a chicory and fennel salad on the side.

———————— • ————————

225g (8oz) fast-cooking polenta or cornmeal
50g (2oz) Gorgonzola cheese, diced

75g (3oz) Fontina, Taleggio, or Brie cheese with rind removed, diced
50g (2oz) butter
salt and freshly ground black pepper

———————— • ————————

1. Prepare the polenta according to the directions on the pack, but don't make it too thick.

2. Add the cheese. As soon as the cheese has melted and blended with the polenta, stir in the butter. Season to taste.

INDEX